DON'T E

DUMBA$$

HOW TO BE SMART IN YOUR TEENS AND TWENTIES AND BECOME A MILLIONAIRE

Adam & Heather
BRUEGGEN

gatekeeper press™
Columbus, Ohio

Don't Be a Dumba$$: How to be Smart in Your Teens and Twenties and Become a Millionaire

Published by Gatekeeper Press
2167 Stringtown Rd, Suite 109
Columbus, OH 43123-2989
www.GatekeeperPress.com

Library of Congress Control Number: 2022945570

ISBN (paperback): 9781662927584
eISBN: 9781662927591

Acknowledgments

We would like to thank the following
individuals for their support and feedback:

Kate McEnerney, Erin Mooney,
Carolyn Lamson, Mark and Lynda Nocera,
Dan Gelatt, Dan Ruttenber, Ciara Moore,
Heather Browne, and Ryan Nelson

Without you, this book would not
have been possible.

"You see, the hard reality is how much money we accumulate in life is not a function of who's President or the economy or bubbles bursting or bad breaks or bosses. It's about the American work ethic. The one that made us the greatest country on Earth. It's about bucking the media's opinion as what constitutes a good parent. Deciding to miss the ball game, the play, the concert because you've resolved to work and invest in your family's future. And taking responsibility for the consequences for those actions. Patience. Frugality. Sacrifice. When you boil it down, what do those three things have in common? Those are choices. Money is not piece of mind. Money is not happiness. **Money is, at its essence, the measure of a man's choices.**" [1] -Marty Byrd, *Ozark*

---

1.   Dubuque, Bill, and Mark Williams. "Ozark: Sugarwood." Episode. *Ozark* 1, no. 1. Netflix, July 21, 2017.

Introduction

The "So What" Factor—Why This Stuff Matters to Me

"My mom told me daily that I would never amount to anything. When I was ten years old, I woke up to my mom standing over me and yelling, 'Get up!' and 'Get outside!' It was chilly, and all I had on were flannel pants and a short-sleeve T-shirt. She proceeded to tell me to lay down on the cold, cement ground. At the time, we lived in a trailer park outside Reno, Nevada. My mom had been diagnosed with manic-depression and was also bipolar, so life with her was always on edge. I never really knew what each day would bring. On this day, my mom decided to ride her bike in circles around me for thirty minutes. She would come as close to me as she could without hitting me, bringing her wheels within inches of running over my head, trying to get me to flinch or move. She screamed at me to 'stay still!' and 'don't get up!' repeatedly. At the time, I remember being cold, shaking, crying, and confused. Why was she doing this? What did I do wrong?

Today, I understand she was trying to control anything or anyone she could because her life was out of control. The problem with her illness is that the life she was experiencing was reality to her, yet utterly different from that of a sane person. I remember thinking, 'Why me? Why was I born to two parents who couldn't get their shit together? Why couldn't I have someone sitting with me *at night to help me with homework? Or making me breakfast in the morning before school? Maybe helping me pick out something for show-and-tell?'*

What was my dad like? My dad, who I saw off and on throughout my life, always talked about how he couldn't wait to make it rich. He always had a million-dollar idea on how to get rich quickly. He made sweatshirts, had a pony business, became an auctioneer, opened a Glamour Shot studio, and even opened a chicken wing restaurant. He never had an actual nine-to-five job.

As a kid, I didn't understand money and how it works, but I did understand that my dad struggled with it and that my mom never had any. Sayings like 'money is tight' were said daily. These money observations combined with my mom's countless maniac episode have one of two outcomes. Outcome #1: Continue to perpetuate the cycle because we are all products of our environment to some extent, or outcome #2: Break the cycle. Change the environment. Make decisions and take action to change the narrative.

*But what about my narrative did I want to change? I knew I wanted a regular job. I knew I wanted to provide any children who I had with a stable home life. I knew I wanted to financially feel safe. Comfortable. Well-off. That was the so-what factor for me. That was the 'so what am I doing all this for every single day?' I needed to feel like everything I went through—all of my struggles, all of my hard work—**was for a reason**.*

*So what was the reason? **To prove to myself that who we become is not determined by our parents, where and how we grow up, our education level, our gender, or our skin color.** Maybe you come from a wealthy family, or maybe you come from* a lower socioeconomic family. Maybe you come from a two-parent household, or maybe you grew up with a single parent who is manic-depressive and bipolar. Maybe you grew up in a high-crime neighborhood, or maybe you grew up in a low-crime area. You get the idea. The point is there is an infinite number of

NOTE TO SELF

"We are not determined by our parents, skin color, education level, or where we grow up. We are determined by the choices we make."

combinations, and no one grows up under the same circumstances. Yet, regardless of their background and upbringing, some succeed while others do not. Why is that? **It's because who you are or who you will become is determined by smart decisions and the grit necessary to make those decisions.** I am living proof of that. If I, someone who had so many odds stacked against me, can become a millionaire, then you, regardless of your situation, can, too. In the end, **I am successful because I decided to be successful**, and I didn't take 'no' for an answer.

You might say to yourself that the decisions we ask you to make are too hard or not for you, and that's fine. But remember, you need money every day no matter what your future may bring you. Everyone has to manage it, at least on a small scale. So, why not aim for the largest scale you can? You're probably also thinking you have so much time, and that you can invest when you are older and have a 'real job.' To be honest, I wish I had started sooner. I wish I had known about the power of investing young sooner. I started investing in my mid-twenties, but even I missed out on my most powerful investing years. Until my mid-twenties, I was **a spender, not an investor,** which cost me dearly. That is my one *regret. Not starting sooner. I try to tell myself that I can't regret what I didn't know. But, you will soon learn about the power of making smart decisions as a teenager and young adult. There is no reason for you to have these same regrets.*

*Was it worth it? In one simple word: yes. All I have to do is imagine where I would be today if I didn't choose hard work and smart decision-making. What if I decided to let society define me? What if I just accepted my life and circumstances as they were that cold morning in the trailer park? I didn't. I made the smart choice. It took having a great partner in life, my husband, to influence me to take it more seriously. It took tapping into my work ethic every day and committing to this process. It took time. It took patience. It wasn't always easy. My parents didn't know it, but with their actions they instilled a work ethic in me that motivates me to show up every single day for myself and my family. To avoid being like my parents and putting my children through the hell I went through. **To never give up. To truly know and understand that I can change my life.***

*I leave you with this: You can't change who you're born to or where you're from, but **you can change who you become, and that's the so-what factor.** The big idea and why all this should matter. To answer the questions, 'What am I going to do?' and 'What outcome do I want?' At the end of the day, what matters is* **how you choose to react to the life you've been given.** *At the end of the day, you decide: 'So, what do I want?'" –Heather*

> **NOTE TO SELF**
>
> You can't change who you're born to or where you're from, but you can change who you become—that's the 'so what' factor.

WHY DO YOU WORK?

Why do I work?

POINT TO PONDER

Let's start by asking you a simple question, "Why do you work?" What motivates you to get out of your bed, get dressed, and go to work… away from your friends and away from doing things that you enjoy? Let's say that today you are in high school or college and went to work and made $60 after your shift was over. After two weeks, you receive your $300 paycheck for working six shifts and use it to buy clothes, eat out, shoes, and gas for your car. The following week, your $300 paycheck is gone. You've heard about investing, but every time you receive your paycheck, you tell yourself, "I'll worry about investing when I get my real job." Fast forward five years, and you finally get your first "real job." After the first two weeks, you log in to your checking account, and there it is—your first "real job" paycheck! It's a lot larger than previous paychecks. You take a second for some self-reflection and tell yourself, "I worked so hard to get here, and for the first time in my life, I am finally making good money and want to enjoy it." So, off you go to enjoy your twenties, and investing is set aside for "another time."

Fast forward to your thirties. You're now married, have two kids, and are earning a higher paycheck but accustomed to a certain lifestyle. Your spending habits have been cemented. At this point, it's hard to change your lifestyle. You haven't thought about investing since starting your job ten years earlier. Investing for your future has been mostly ignored, but your expenses are now higher than they were before. Vacations, kids' sports events, groceries, camps, gym memberships, a mortgage, two car payments, and daycare all add up. You are still not investing. Okay, now you're fifty and are still doing the same thing… vacations, cars, clothes… another decade of financial neglect. Blink, and you're sixty. Both kids have gone on to college, your body starts to ache, your knees get sore after running, and your back hurts after raking leaves in the fall. Work is not as fun as it once was. You're tired.

Meanwhile, most of your friends are now living their best lives retired, traveling to Florida and Arizona every winter to relax in warmer weather. They have ample money saved up to eat out whenever they want and travel wherever they want. However, not you. You always focused on your immediate needs and you ignored one important thing: *your future*. You have money in your employer's 401K and equity in your house. Heck, you can soon collect social security. But that is not enough. Health care insurance alone can cost thousands a month in your fifties to mid-sixties. At this point, living your life without financial consequences has finally hit you. You realize that *you will have to work for the rest of your life because you can't afford NOT to work*. Your optimism for the future and the idea that there is still time have all been shattered. Tomorrow, next month, and next year have now become *today*.

Sadly, the above scenario is all too common. According to the Natixis Global Retirement Index, 41% of Americans, or roughly two out of five adults, say it will take a miracle to retire.[2] But, if not taken seriously, the story you just read could be a sneak peek into *your future*.

---

2.   Dickler, Jessica. "41% Of Americans Say It's 'Going to Take a Miracle' to Be Ready for Retirement, Report Finds." CNBC, September 14, 2021. https://www.cnbc.com/2021/09/14/36percent-of-americans-say-they-wont-have-enough-to-retire-report-finds.html.

Now, let's go back to the original question: Why do you work? Yes, *part of the reason* you work is to buy your Starbucks, pay your car payment, and shop on Amazon. However, the *main reason* you work is *so one day you don't have to.*

NOTE TO SELF

The main reason you work is so one day you don't have to.

WHO ARE TODAY'S MILLIONAIRES?

Let's start out by examining who today's millionaires are, where they came from, and how they got there. Did you know that 88% of American millionaires are self-made or made it on their own?[3] They did not inherit it, win the lottery, or hit it big in Vegas. More importantly, eight out of ten millionaires came from the *middle or lower* classes.[4] This means that despite what you may have read or seen on TV, most millionaires started like you and us. This stat is also powerful because it confirms that becoming a millionaire is achievable for anyone *regardless of where they start out in life*. Like many of you, today's millionaires most likely started out waiting tables, cashiering at retail stores, or flipping burgers. But how did they go from being a high school student with no investments to a millionaire? They made smart life choices in their teens and twenties that set them apart from their peers. *They also wanted it more than others* and *worked harder to achieve it*. What happened to everyone else?

---

3.   Sightings, Tom. "7 Myths about Millionaires." U.S. News, November 29, 2018. https://money.usnews.com/money/blogs/on-retirement/articles/7-myths-about-millionaires.

4.   Ramsey Solutions. "The National Study of Millionaires." Ramsey Solutions, May 6, 2022. https://www.ramseysolutions.com/retirement/the-national-study-of-millionaires-research.

WHY DO AMERICANS STRUGGLE WITH FINANCES?

There are two main reasons why Americans struggle with finances. First, *finances are not a priority in the American education system, culture, and, many times, at home.* When was the last time you saw James Bond speeding away from the villain driving a 2014 Toyota Camry? Or listening to a Grammy Award Winning Artist sing about her Roth IRA? The education system puts little emphasis on a subject that every student deals with multiple times a day: money. At the time of this writing, only fourteen of the fifty US states mandate personal finance as a requirement for high school graduation.[5] Since money is not adequately taught in most schools, high school graduates enter their post-high school lives with very little knowledge of navigating critical decisions that will have life-lasting financial impacts.

Thus, it's no wonder why so many Americans are financially lost because many start adulthood somewhat clueless about what to do. As a result, many high school graduates lack basic financial awareness and waste their most valuable investment years (their teens and twenties). Sure, they

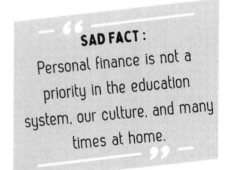

SAD FACT:
Personal finance is not a priority in the education system, our culture, and many times at home.

graduate understanding reading, writing, and arithmetic but lack sufficient knowledge to apply their education to real life. Finances are the boring reality that no one wants to talk about but are needed

---

5.   Reinicke, Carmen. "Michigan Officially Becomes 14th State to Mandate Personal Finance Education Before High School Graduation." CNBC, June 16, 2022. https://www.cnbc.com/2022/06/16/michigan-becomes-14th-state-to-mandate-personal-finance-education.html.

daily. This lack of financial education has devastating results. In 2016, Standard and Poor's, a US financial ratings company, found that only 57% of adults are financially literate.[6] Or said another way, *43% of adults are not financially literate.* How can we, as a society, expect adults to succeed when 43% are not financially literate?

Before we go any further, it's important to understand that high academic achievement does not guarantee high levels of wealth, nor does low or average academic achievement prevent you from high levels of wealth. Being "money smart" has little do with academic achievement because academics and successful money habits have little in common. Instead, money-smart is attitude and mindset.

DID YOU KNOW?

In 2018, 78% of Americans lived paycheck-to-paycheck.
The median salary was $65,712 and the poverty line for a family of four was $25,701.
What's going on with the other $40,011?
Data From US Census Bureau

The second reason Americans struggle with finances is corporate marketing has programmed and brainwashed society to be obsessed with materialism. *Americans don't have a money problem; Americans have a spending problem.* It is ingrained in our culture. We are bombarded with messages every day telling us to spend money. It's nearly impossible to watch a TV show, football game, or YouTube video

---

6.   Smith, Kelly Anne. "These States Now Require Students To Learn About Personal Finance." Forbes Advisor, April 1, 2022. https://www.forbes.com/advisor/personal-finance/states-mandating-personal-finance-in-school/.

without seeing advertisements. We are constantly told that we need the newest phone, the designer brand clothes, the fancy house, or the new car to be happy. Unfortunately, marketing is compelling, making many feel like they MUST spend money, and sometimes, more than they have. To be clear, we are not telling you that you should not spend your money. Consumerism does make the world go 'round, after all. But part of every paycheck should be set aside for your financial future, especially in your teens and twenties.

WHO WE ARE

We are a couple who are financially self-taught, have used our money wisely, and wish to impart our tips and tricks to the next generation.

Adam grew up in Wisconsin in a middle-class family. After high school, he joined the Army National Guard and later joined the Air Force's Reserve Officer Training Corps program at the University of Wisconsin on an electrical engineering scholarship. He graduated from college with no debt, was commissioned as a Second Lieutenant in the United States Air Force, and has continued serving ever since. Adam credits joining the military to pay for his college and *graduating debt-free as the most significant enabler of his financial success*. By graduating debt-free, he was able to max out his Roth Individual Retirement Account (IRA) annually and put additional investment money in non-retirement investments immediately after college.

Adam's investment ambitions began because he wanted to own deer-hunting land. He told a family friend about his wish, and the family friend challenged him by saying, "You better start saving up because it will likely cost at least half a million dollars." At the time, Adam was twenty years old with big ambitions to own hunting land but had no money and no plan. Determined to succeed, he brainstormed ways to get enough money to buy his land. Today, that seed of desire and ambition has allowed him to save enough money to buy that hunting property.

Heather brings a very different perspective with her unsteady childhood. She grew up near poverty, temporarily lived in a car, and, as you already know,

FAKE NEWS
Most millionaires come from rich parents.

had a mom who suffered from severe mental health disorders. Once when she was thirteen, Heather came home from school to an empty house and a note from her mom stating she would be away for a few weeks. Alone and with no cell phone or nearby family, she quickly learned how to be self-sufficient. She took the bus to school each day, did her homework, and made her meals until all that was left was a loaf of bread and a jar of peanut butter. Seven weeks passed. To survive so young and with no money, Heather had to ask her neighbors for food. At this point, Heather didn't know that she would never see her mother again. On that day, alone and worried about how she would survive, Heather *made the decision and became determined to end her cycle of poverty and never be that scared, hungry girl again.* She later attended the University of Nevada, Las Vegas, majored in secondary education, and is currently a high school teacher. Her childhood financial struggles drove her ambitions. Today, she has created a life of financial independence for herself and her family.

Why does this matter? Because we both come from different backgrounds. Adam was motivated to own hunting land and understood *that smart life choices led to better outcomes and increased his chances for success.* Heather overcame personal hardships and never let them define who she was or would become. *That tenacity and grit influenced her life choices*, making her a stable and successful woman today. The philosophies and principles outlined in this book are attainable and achievable for any young adult willing to make smart decisions.

WHY DID WE WRITE THIS BOOK?

This book was written for two reasons. First, to properly educate young adults on money, a topic that is used daily. Second, to deprogram everything corporate marketing has brainwashed you into believing and to reprogram with necessary, life-lasting financial knowledge. More than likely, you, too, are not adequately prepared for life's financial dilemmas and know very little about what decisions are needed to transition your classroom education to financial independence. It's alarming to see the number of deer-in-headlights looks we get when talking about finances with young adults. Whether you become a nurse, engineer, teacher, salesman, or electrician, you must know how to manage money. We want to provide you with the knowledge that creates a life of financial freedom. Being a millionaire is NOT impossible and is not just for celebrities and doctors. It *is obtainable to anyone who makes smart decisions while young,* and this book was written to empower you to become one. You cannot control 100% of any outcome, but *you can control 100% of the decisions made in your life.* You are in the driver's seat of your life and are the Chief

NOTE TO SELF

> You cannot control 100% of any outcome, but you can control 100% of the decisions made in your life.

Executive Officer (CEO) on every decision. Ultimately, it is up to you and only you to make it happen.

Our mission is to ensure more young adults have a prosperous future by teaching them to be financially independent. But unfortunately, there is a disservice in society that places little emphasis on money management that continues crippling future generations. It's time to even the playing field.

WHY IS THE BOOK TITLED "DON'T BE A DUMBA$$"?

When we brainstormed titles for this book, we wanted something encompassing the "secret" to becoming a millionaire. It dawned on us that the secret is simple: Don't be a dumba$$, especially in your teens and twenties. You're probably thinking to yourself, "I'm getting good grades and have a plan for what I'm doing after high school. I'm not a dumba$$." Well, that's great; however, when we say "dumba$$," we are not referring to your book smarts or academic aptitude. Instead, we are talking about your *attitude* and *mindset*. For example, if you have a job but are not investing some of your paycheck, you are a dumba$$. To be clear, being a dumba$$ has *nothing* to do with your grades, SAT/ACT scores, whether or not you went to college, where you are or will go to college, or any other academic achievements, but has everything to do with your attitude and mindset.

FAKE NEWS
I am not smart enough to become a millionaire.

While some might take this phrase offensively, the truth is this: The American capitalistic system is set up and ready for *anyone* who wants to be a millionaire. Unfortunately, this "invisible system" is not a priority in schools, is not advertised on billboards, and is not the subject of the most popular TikTok videos. But, at the end of the day, it is that simple. The system is already set up for you. All you have to do is show up, follow some basic instructions, and don't be a dumba$$.

HOW IS THIS BOOK DIFFERENT FROM OTHERS, AND WHY SHOULD YOU READ IT?

This book is different from other financial books because we are *not* financial professionals. You may be a bit puzzled why you are reading a financial book written by non-financial professionals. By the end of the book, you'll realize that a financial professional is a misleading term because they do not outperform or have a higher return than the broad American stock market in the long run. To be financially successful, six critical decisions must be made, and these have little to do with your GPA or where you went to college. These six decisions are discussed in detail in this book.

By not being financial professionals, we are relatable. Heather is a high school teacher, and Adam is an Air Force officer. Even though neither of us went to business school, w*e are experts* in making every day, smart decisions young adults can make to become millionaires, which is what really matters. We are also experts in the mindset and attitude needed to make it happen, which you will see is more important than any degree or GPA. We both started with nothing, including the knowledge of how to start. We began by working minimum wage jobs without a single penny in any investment account. Adam worked at McDonald's and Orange Julius, and Heather served at the International House of Pancakes (IHOP). We worked hard, made smart decisions, and have the scars to prove it. Yet, with no formal finance or investing education, we became millionaires at thirty-three. *You can too.*

We're not going to throw out buzzwords or catchphrases, nor lecture you to "eat your vegetables." Instead, we walk you through everyday decisions many of you have or will soon face and the financial impacts, or what we will later call the second- and third-order effects. The book includes realistic scenarios, real-life stories, advice, and, most importantly, the financial consequences that are often ignored. Hopefully, by the end of the book, you will understand why you should make smart decisions *now* and not in ten years.

This book is a *preemptive* financial book because we want you to think critically *before making major life decisions.* Many decisions made in your teens and twenties have life-lasting financial consequences, and we will coach you on how to avoid costly pitfalls and mistakes. This is not a financial self-help book because self-help implies someone is already in financial distress, which we want you to avoid in the first place.

The book's process, information, and strategies worked for us and can be applied to your life. Being a millionaire boils down to something so obvious that often people forget how impactful they are: *smart decisions.* In these pages, we examine and discuss what we consider to be the six biggest decisions that impact your financial future. These decisions are timeless;

NOTE TO SELF

"You are where you are today because of decisions made in the past."

they are just as relevant today as they were fifty years ago and will also be relevant fifty years from now when your grandkids are trying to follow in your footsteps. To be clear, this is not the end-all-be-all money management and investment book, but it provides basic concepts and principles that many young Americans can emulate.

WHAT TO EXPECT IN THIS BOOK

Expect to learn that making smart decisions is paramount to becoming a millionaire. Every good decision gets you one step closer to being a millionaire, while a bad decision can take you many steps away. You can *choose* to buy a used car rather than a new one. You can *choose* to invest or spend your money. You can *choose* to make smart decisions or be a dumba$$. Of course, there are exceptions to every situation. We understand not everything in life is in your control, like losing your job or having a medical emergency. However, in that case, isn't it more important to make informed decisions on things *you can control*? Most importantly, it starts while you are young with a clean slate and before you make poor life choices that will have negative financial consequences later in life.

Remember this key point: *You are where you are today because of decisions you made in the past.* Today's success or failure, for the most part, can be traced to past decisions. No one wakes up one morning as a millionaire but instead achieves it by making a series of good decisions over a period of time. At the same time, no one wakes up one morning in bad financial shape but instead gets there by making a series of poor decisions over a period of time. Bottom line, if you want to be or achieve something *in the future*, good decision-making *today and going forward* is paramount.

For the most part, your road to being a millionaire comes down to your decisions determined by three primary inputs: *when you start, how much you invest, and what you invest in.* All these elements are *in your control*, and *only you can make it happen.* The six decisions that drive these three inputs in this book are shown in the graphic.

Each decision has its chapter and is more thoroughly discussed later in the book. Making smart choices is not impossible because everyone can make smart life choices. If everyone can make smart choices, then everyone can be a millionaire. *Being a millionaire does not come down to your intellect; it primarily depends on behavior and mindset,* which revolves around the book's six essential decisions to secure your financial future.

To summarize, we wrote this book to convince you to change your behavior and help deprogram any bad money management behavior you may have been taught. Essentially, we want to help preemptively alter how you approach money and change any bad attitude you may have about money before it begins to have life-lasting ripple effects. We are here to convince you that anyone can be a millionaire. It comes down to your behavior and your mindset. It comes down to *your* choices. It comes down to your ambition. *Human ambition is an amazing quality because we all have the capacity for greatness,* but it starts *with you.* So let's change the narrative that many Americans have a spending problem to a narrative that Americans have *an investing* problem. The legendary investor Warren Buffet once said, "It is not necessary to do extraordinary things to get extraordinary results."[7] You do not need to do extraordinary things. But with some guidance and a shift in behavior and mindset, you can achieve extraordinary results; just don't be a dumba$$!

NOTE TO SELF

66 Making smart choices is not impossible; everyone can make smart life choices. 99

---

7.   "Warren Buffett Quote: 'It Is Not Necessary to Do Extraordinary Things to Get Extraordinary Results.'" Quotefancy. https://quotefancy.com/quote/931132/Warren-Buffett-It-is-not-necessary-to-do-extraordinary-things-to-get-extraordinary.

DECISION 1:
MAKE IT YOUR GOAL

"Setting goals is the first step in turning the invisible to visible."
-Tony Robbins

"I remember the day Adam and I decided to write this book. It was sometime in November 2020, and I had just gotten home from running errands. Adam was home with the kids. When I walked in, he was FaceTiming with his sister and giving her advice on what to invest her 401K in. While FaceTiming and discussing investments is not exactly an everyday expectation for most families, this is just another day in the Brueggen household. Adam is ALWAYS giving financial advice to anyone willing to listen. He has even tried convincing our five-year-old to put his allowance in a mutual fund instead of buying a toy. Anyway, the phone call ended, and I said to him, 'You should write a financial advice book for young adults,' jokingly. However, he thought about it for a second, took my suggestion to heart, and the rest is history.

At the time, we were living in Montgomery, Alabama, and Adam was a student at the Air Force's Air Command and Staff College, where his days were consumed by lectures, seminars, reading over one hundred pages a day, and writing numerous research papers. Writing a book on finances, a subject as exciting as watching paint dry, that connects with teenagers and young adults who have little to no interest in learning about it, is no small feat. After all, deprogramming some teenagers or young adults who may have consistently been told by society that they need a nice car or expensive clothes to get 'the girl' is next to impossible.

*The pandemic was in full swing, and we had three young kids who required our near-constant attention from the time they woke up early in the morning until the time they went to bed. Where in the world would Adam find time to write a book? What did he even know about writing a book? Adam always enjoyed helping people with their finances and had always talked about writing a book 'one day.' But this was the day he decided to no longer dream of writing a book but decided to make it his **goal**.*

*At first, it was mostly Adam writing about whatever was on his mind late into the night and me proofreading. Then it evolved into something that became a message from the two of us. We were deeply committed to changing how young adults view finances and felt a sense of purpose to help others. It soon turned into an obsession and became our passion. It became **our** goal.*

The road to writing this book was not easy. Along the way, we hit many bumps. Early on, one person said it wasn't any good. Other people have said it's similar to other money management books. Regardless, and not to be discouraged, we stayed committed, made changes to make it better, and kept going. No matter what life threw at us, we always found a way to keep working. At times, one of us would work on it at a coffee shop while the other stayed behind with the kids. We stayed up into the early morning hours after the kids had gone to bed too often to recall. I worked on it several times while sitting in a parked car in an empty neighborhood parking lot just to get a few undisturbed hours from Adam and the kids. Adam would constantly send text messages to me with a good idea that popped into his head at all hours of the day. Sometimes at three in the morning. Adam even wrote the back of the book section on his iPhone while sitting in a tree stand with his bow in the other hand, occasionally looking up for deer. Writing, reading, editing, writing, rereading, editing, and reading it… again… again… making sure every sentence and every word was perfect—and of course, nothing ever is.

*This **goal**, writing this book, has encompassed our lives, and we have sacrificed a lot in doing so. We had to preserve. We had to face and overcome many challenges. Each time, we readjusted and came back stronger. But that is the point of a goal. To work towards it every single day. Some days are better than others. Some days we wanted to give up, while other days thought we were onto something great. Maybe the book will flop, maybe it'll sell a few copies, who knows? But the point is, we set out to reach a **goal** and will see it through to the end. **It hasn't been easy, but we never gave up**. Hopefully, this book will motivate and help many young Americans become millionaires, as Adam has always wanted, which will have made all of our sacrifices worth it." –Heather*

Decision 1: make becoming a millionaire your goal. You now have a clear and defined purpose by making it a goal. People find strength in goals because goals are the foundation for something greater. What is that something greater? It's the motivation you need to stay focused on your goal. And, without a goal, nothing matters because you aren't driven to achieve anything.

Becoming a millionaire is a straightforward strategy that is a function of three primary inputs: *when you start, how much you invest, and what you invest in*. These elements are in your control, and only you can make them happen. These inputs are the action plan for your goal. So, this chapter's main takeaway is: If you don't want to be a dumba$$, **make being a millionaire your goal**.

WHAT IS A GOAL?

You have all heard the word "goal." However, it is usually said in passing with some bit of "I have to ask you this" tone, such as, "What are your goals?", "How do you plan to get there?", and "What do you want to be when you grow up?" In response, many people rattle off some sort of stereotypical answer. But here's the thing, goals

> " Tough times never last, but tough people do. -Robert Schuller "

are so much more than answering a question on a "get to know you" form or writing about it on your college applications. Goals are what drive us. They drive us to be better versions of ourselves. They drive us to get up in the morning and do better than the day before. *They drive us to achieve our dreams.*

With that, let's discuss the difference between dreams and goals. There is a stark difference between saying, "I dream of being a millionaire," versus, "My goal is to be a millionaire." So what is it?

> **NOTE TO SELF**
> " Goals drive us to be better versions of ourselves. "

Let's first answer, "What is a dream?" A dream is something you want, but it's often a thought that many don't take action on. *To dream is simple.* You let your mind wander without any real outcome. What is a goal? A goal is the desired outcome achieved by completing steps or events beforehand. The important difference is that a goal is action-oriented with measurable steps, and you have to work for it. You either succeed or fail. You either lose ten pounds or you don't. You either win the football game or you don't. You either become a millionaire or you don't. Goals motivate you to act. They provide a reason. Thus, dreams are goals *without* an action or a plan, and a goal is a dream *with* an action or a plan. If you *actually* want to be a millionaire, you have to make it a goal, not just a dream. As a goal, you need an action-oriented plan to turn your dream into reality.

Now, we want to ask you, "Do *you* want to be a millionaire?" and, more importantly, "Are you willing to work for it?" While you are pondering your answer, ask yourself if you want to someday live in a bigger house, drive a nicer car, and have more financial freedom to do the things you enjoy. Of course, nearly everyone wants to be a millionaire, *but do you have the determination, patience, and self-control to stick to a plan until your goal is achieved?*

We get it; goals can be intimidating. Some goals seem like they will never happen regardless of the plan. Working to become a millionaire may make you feel like you are standing at the base of a tall, intimidating mountain looking up. Maybe some people have told you that you will never get to the top of the mountain. Rest assured, there is a top to the mountain. You can reach it. You simply must climb it one step at a time by *making one smart decision over and over.*

What makes *you* different from others who want to be a millionaire? You may not realize it, but you are the *ideal candidate* with the highest probability of becoming one because you are young. You have a clean slate and have not made the financial mistakes some older adults may have made.

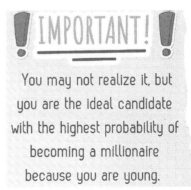

IMPORTANT!

You may not realize it, but you are the ideal candidate with the highest probability of becoming a millionaire because you are young.

Most importantly, you have the best weapon *in your* arsenal, time, and a *lot of it*. To put this into perspective using a military analogy, prospective millionaires in their teens and twenties are going into battle armed with a tank, while prospective millionaires in their forties and fifties are going into battle armed with bows and arrows. As a result, younger people are better equipped, which gives them a distinct advantage over everyone else.

DID YOU KNOW?

Someone in their forties with no investments will have to invest almost five times more a month than someone in their twenties to become a millionaire. Someone in their fifties with no investments will have to invest ten times more.

While your mountain may seem steep and high, someone looking at climbing the mountain in their forties and fifties has a substantially steeper mountain to climb—for some, they can't even see the top! The journey is not easy, no matter who does it; however, contrary to popular opinion, *becoming a millionaire is most achievable by starting in your teens and twenties*—in other words, *starting while young provides the highest probability of achieving it.*

To reach your goal, follow these four steps:

Step 1: Identify your goal. Goals come in all shapes and sizes. Since you are reading this book, your goal is likely to be a millionaire. Regardless, you must identify what it is to begin working towards it. After that, write it down and place it somewhere as a daily reminder—

your refrigerator, a bathroom mirror. Your goal needs to be measurable and obtainable.

Step 2: Plan it out. Identify the actions or steps needed to achieve it. Becoming a millionaire doesn't just happen. You don't just randomly wake up one day a millionaire. It is achieved by following a well-thought-out plan over time.

Step 3: Execute. Next, follow your plan and make it happen. During execution, the most important attributes are willpower and determination to stick to your plan day-in and day-out, year after year, until your goal is reached.

Step 4: Monitor your plan and make adjustments. Regularly evaluate and assess your progress and make adjustments if needed. The path to becoming a millionaire is not a straight line, and you will experience setbacks during your climb to the top. A job loss, a large stock market decline, or a bad relationship are a few examples of life events that will most likely set you back. When a setback does occur, reevaluate, make adjustments and continue towards your destiny.

SHORT-SIGHTEDNESS

Throughout our time writing this book, we have enjoyed talking with high school and college-aged students about their future. Of

OPERATION DON'T BE A DUMBA$$

Your Mission:
Use short and long-term goals to plan how to become a millionaire.

course, a common topic is talking about their goals. Many young adults quickly rattle off their intended major, the college they were accepted to, a program they plan to attend, or maybe a job they will start working the day they graduate. It's great to know young adults are looking ahead and thinking about their futures. However, what has become apparent is that many young adults *only have short-term goals.* Or at least that is what they easily discuss. We have yet to talk to someone who mentions anything past a few years post-high school, much less their long-term goals. *Short-term goals support long-term goals.* Not to say that young adults don't think about these things. Maybe they do. But we highly doubt that the average eighteen-year-old has figured out how much money they will need to retire. Or how much their college loan payment will be. The point is it's important to focus on both short- and long-term goals. College and your first job are important but then what's next? What does your major or college enable you to do? Most likely, you are going to live to be at least eighty. Most college graduates are either twenty-two or twenty-three years of age and *still have 70% of their life left after college.* So, keep focusing on post-high school education or jobs, but don't forget to tie that into your long-term plans.

DID YOU KNOW?

After college, you still have about 70% of your life left to live.

KEY TAKEAWAYS OF DECISION 1:

- Goals are what drives us to achieve our dreams
- Goals are action-oriented and measurable
- Make becoming a millionaire a goal and not a dream
- Without action, drive, and persistence, a goal is just a dream

In summary, why is the first decision on becoming a millionaire addressing goals and dreams? Because becoming a millionaire takes time and discipline, and it is important to understand the difference between making it your goal to be a millionaire and dreaming of becoming a millionaire. A goal provides motivation and purpose. If your goal is to be a millionaire, a well-thought-out plan is needed because a million dollars will not just appear in your bank account one morning. More important than the plan is having the willpower to see it through. Commitment is needed every day, *not just when it's convenient*. Without action, drive, and persistence, it's just a dream. It is just a moment when you dream of better things, dream of financial security, and dream of being a millionaire. Don't just dream. Take action, and *you will achieve your goal*.

Decision 2: Invest Young

"I made my first investment at age 11. I was wasting my life up until then."
-Warren Buffet

"I started working at sixteen as a server at an International House of Pancakes (IHOP) in Las Vegas, where I averaged $2,200 a month in tips. At twenty-one, I left IHOP and worked at Buffalo Wild Wings (BWW) for five years, where I averaged $3,200 a month in tips. Then at age twenty-three, I also began teaching and had a starting salary of $28,656. During this period, I had minimal living expenses, and like most teens and college kids, I spent most of my money on anything I wanted. Cars. Clothes. Eating Out. Traveling. Everything. I estimate that I made roughly $409,000 between the ages of sixteen and twenty-five but never invested a dime. **Today my $409,000 is worth $0. Zero dollars.** It's almost like I never worked because **I have nothing to show for it today**. One thing that is certain is I made a lot of other people and companies rich by buying their stuff but didn't do anything to make myself rich. Simply put, I was a dumba$$.

Where did it all go? To be honest, I don't recall everything, but whatever stuff that I bought throughout my teens and early twenties wasn't important enough that I remember or still have today. I regret that not one penny went towards my future. That is NINE years that I can't get back financially. I admit that I wonder what if I invested 25% of my pre-tax income instead of spending it? What would it be worth today, and what would it be worth at age sixty, assuming an 8% annual return?

Job	Age	Monthly Income	Monthly Investment	Annual Investment	Value at age 37	Value at 60
IHOP	16-21	$2,200	$550	$6,600	$143,263	$841,164
BWW	21-25	$3,200	$800	$9,600	$141,822	$832,701
Teacher	23-25	$2,388	$597	$7,164	$58,566	$343,866
Total				**$102,492**	**$343,651**	**$2,017,731**

Table 1. Heather's Financial Projection

*The table above shows that if I had invested 25% of my money, then **time, the most powerful weapon in one's investing arsenal,** would have transformed my $102,492 investment into $343,651 today and $2,017,731 at sixty. Had I known about the power of investing young and invested before getting my real job, **I could have never worked again after twenty-five and still been worth over two million dollars at age sixty from waiting tables and filling drinks.***

I admit that the 'what if' number is hard to look at. But, I remind myself that I didn't know any better. I didn't know that if I invested young, in my case when I was sixteen, I would not only be a millionaire but a multi-millionaire. I regularly hear from high school and college students that they will invest

when they get their 'real job.' But here's the deal: Whether you invest some of your part-time high school or college paycheck, or your 'real job' money, it all counts. However, **investments made with your part-time high school and college jobs are more powerful than your real job because of the extra time.** The difference that four *or five additional years invested make in your financial future is mind-blowing, as you'll soon read about in this chapter. Getting an additional four or five investment years can only be achieved by investing before your 'real job.'*

*I never realized that I had a choice of what to do with my money. **I always assumed you earn money to spend money**. I didn't know you could do something with your money other than spending it all or putting it in a savings account. I didn't know the power of investing young and didn't know how much waiting a few years would cost me. I wasted roughly $409,000 on stuff that I no longer own or can barely recall what I bought. When you're in your teens and twenties, it feels like life is eternal and that there will always be time later to save, to invest, and to plan for your future, but if this story proves anything, it is this: **Waiting to invest will end up costing you a lot of money or in my case, Two Million**."*
–Heather

At this point, you have committed to becoming a millionaire as your goal. Great! The first and sometimes the hardest step, committing to a long-term endeavor, is done. What's next? The second step and one that gives you the highest probability of becoming a millionaire is investing young. No other decision comes close. *We began investing in our early twenties, which is a major factor in why we are millionaires today.*

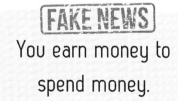

FAKE NEWS
You earn money to spend money.

As we've stated before, becoming a millionaire is a straightforward strategy that is a function of three primary inputs: *when you start, how much you invest, and what you invest in*. These elements are in your control, and only you can make them happen. The first input, when you start, is thoroughly explained in this chapter. While investing young is not

mandatory to become a millionaire, *it is the easiest and surest way to become one regardless of one's profession*; however, every year that investing is delayed makes it harder to achieve. For the most part, failing to invest in your twenties could cut your lifetime net worth by almost 50%. It can be the difference between one million dollars and two, four million and eight. So, this chapter's main takeaway is: If you don't want to be a dumba$$, **invest young**.

This chapter's purpose is to explain *why* investing young is so critical on your journey to becoming a millionaire. It does not talk about *how* and *what to invest in*. Investment strategies are addressed in Chapter 6.

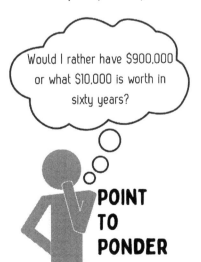

Would I rather have $900,000 or what $10,000 is worth in sixty years?

POINT TO PONDER

Before we begin, we'd like to ask you a question: Would you rather have $900,000, or what $10,000 would be worth in sixty years with an 8% return? Take a second and think about the question and your choice. Then, hold on to it because we'll revisit the question at the end of the chapter.

TIME: YOUR MOST POWERFUL WEAPON IN INVESTING

Time is your most powerful weapon in investing due to compound growth. It can be more powerful than your career and, in many instances, how much you make. Compound growth accelerates an investment's return as time progresses, meaning your return gets higher and higher with each passing year. The growth

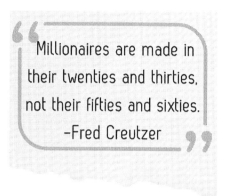

Millionaires are made in their twenties and thirties, not their fifties and sixties.
–Fred Creutzer

accelerates because an investment grows not only by the return or how much money was made from the initial investment, but also from the return of all the previous year's gains, distributions, and dividends *combined.*

To make sure we're on the same page, *gains* are how much money your account is up. In contrast, *distributions* are money paid to you, the shareholder, after a fund manager (person running an investment) makes a profitable sale on an asset that he or she is managing. A fund's distributions are usually reinvested in more shares of the investment. Finally, *dividends* are a portion of a company's earnings paid directly to the shareholder in cash and are typically expressed as a percent. For example, an investment with a 2% dividend pays its shareholders 2% of the money invested. So, a $1,000 investment with a 2% dividend pays $20 in dividends every year.

The initial investment, gains, distributions, and dividends all work together to cause the investment's growth to accelerate as time progresses. In other words, this year's growth is faster than last year's, and next year's growth will be faster than this year's. Kevin O'Leary, also known as Mr. Wonderful on the popular TV show *Shark Tank*, has a quote about making money which also describes compound growth well: "Here's how I think of money: soldiers. I send them out to war every day. I want them to take prisoners and come home, so there's more of them."[8] Let's say that today, his army has ten soldiers. They go out to war and come home with two prisoners, and the army has now grown to twelve soldiers. Tomorrow, those twelve soldiers go out and come back with three prisoners and have grown to fifteen soldiers. And so forth. As each period passes, the army grows larger and at a faster rate because the soldiers and prisoners work together to grow larger. The same can be said about investing. Like soldiers, your money grows larger and faster as time passes. Therefore, the more time, the more your money grows. To visually see how compound growth works, let's look at how $10,000 grows over five years.

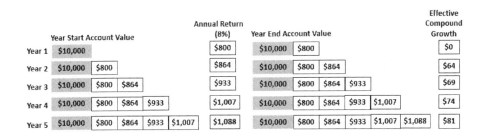

Table 2. Compound Growth Example

Each year, the annual return goes up by 8% on not only the initial $10,000 but on *all previous annual increases combined*. For example, Year 5's annual return of $1,088 is a function of the initial $10,000 investment and Years 1 through 4's combined annual returns. After 40 years, an investment's gain is a function of Year 1 through 39's combined annual returns. Basically, compound growth causes your account balance to

8.   O'Leary, Kevin. "Kevin O'Leary: Money as Soldiers." Made of Money, June 4, 2021. https://itsamoneything.com/money/kevin-oleary-money-as-soldiers/.

make money, and that money then makes more money, and then all that money together makes even more money, and so forth. *The longer it's invested, the more powerful it becomes.*

In Table 2, compound growth is captured in the Effective Compound Growth column on the right. That column shows the amount of compound growth in that year's annual return. For example, $64 of the $864 annual return in Year 2 is compound growth. The table also shows how growth increases faster with each passing year. For example, there was a $5 increase in compound growth between Years 2 and 3 and a $7 increase between Years 4 and 5.

A great visual example of compound growth in action is a snowball going down a hill. In the beginning, the snowball (your initial investment) is small, but as it goes downhill, it grows bigger and becomes more powerful the farther it travels. Like compound growth, the initial snowball and the added snow work *together* to make the snowball grow. The bigger the snowball gets, the faster it grows. With enough time, a once-small snowball (initial investment) can easily turn into a gigantic snowball (a million dollars or more). The longer your money is invested, the more it will be worth. Bottom line: *Time transforms a small amount of money into A LOT of money.*

NOTE TO SELF

❝ Time transforms a small amount of money into a lot of money and is your most powerful weapon. ❞

PAYING YOURSELF FIRST-THE FIRST MINDSET CHANGE NEEDED

Money management teaches a valuable life lesson that changes your behavior and mindset to acquire money-saving habits and discipline. One of the essential money management lessons is this: *When you buy something, you are making someone else rich.* Likewise, *when you invest, you make yourself rich.* Doing the latter is known as paying yourself first or allocating money from your paycheck and investing it. For example, if you earn $2,000 a paycheck, pay yourself first by investing $200 or some other amount you can afford. To be a millionaire, paying yourself first must be a priority and a habit.

NOTE TO SELF

66 When I buy something, I make someone else rich. When I invest, I make myself rich. 99

We are what you might consider "millionaires next door."[9] A millionaire next door is a phrase used to describe someone who doesn't act like a millionaire based on where they live, what they drive, how they dress, or how they act. We both have government jobs and earn the same salaries as anyone else in our profession with the same work

OPERATION DON'T BE A DUMBA$$

Your Mission:
Always pay yourself first and invest as young as possible.

---

9.   Stanley, Thomas J., and William D. Danko. The Millionaire next Door: *The Surprising Secrets of America's Wealthy.* Lanham: Taylor Trade Publishing, 1996.

experience. What makes us financially exceptional is our decisions and willingness to always pay ourselves first. Of course, paying yourself first looks different for everyone. From the beginning, we did everything to minimize our expenses. We drove older, paid-off cars, ate out using Groupon specials, found free or inexpensive ways to have fun such as going to playgrounds and hiking, and we bought used when practical. Multiple *decisions that result in a $10 savings here and there add up to hundreds of dollars each month, which can easily make the difference between "paying yourself first" and not.*

Adam drove a 2007 Nissan Sentra until May 2021. Just before we got rid of it, it had faded paint, stains on the back seats, a non-functioning front window, 195,000 miles, smelled like dogs, and the hood did not close properly. Basically, a teenager wouldn't be caught dead driving it. Adam's mom frequently told him that he was an "Air Force officer and shouldn't drive a car like that." However, ignoring her advice, he continued driving it. We finally got rid of it when we couldn't physically take the car to one of our military assignments. There's no question that if we didn't have to move, he'd still be happily driving it today. Why? Because the car did its purpose and got him safely from point A to point B. He always said, "Why sell a paid-off car if it still does the job it was supposed to do?" Sure, the car may not have turned heads, but it was a money machine because it was paid off. Because it was paid off, the old, reliable Sentra, like clockwork, kept doing its intended

DID YOU KNOW?

Investing $400 a year from birth to age eighteen ($7,200 total) is worth roughly the same as investing $3,600 a year from age thirty to sixty ($180,000 total).

purpose of driving its passengers safely from point A to point B. This allowed us to invest $285 monthly which would have otherwise gone to a car payment for eight years. This $285 monthly investment made over eight years will turn into $230,675 at age sixty.

AN S&P 500 INDEX FUND–THE SIMPLEST AND BEST INVESTMENT

All investment examples throughout this book are invested in an S&P 500 Index Fund, which is an investment that replicates the performance and composition of the S&P 500 Index. The S&P 500 Index is comprised of America's 500 largest companies, including Microsoft, McDonald's, Amazon, Walmart, Tesla, Apple, Nike, Starbucks, and Home Depot, to name a few. So essentially, it is a superfund invested in the US's 500 largest companies. In addition, all examples assume an 8% annual return because that has been the S&P 500 Index's historical annual return.[10] Finally, unless noted otherwise, none of the examples factor in taxation, mutual fund fees, and inflation effects for simplicity's sake. However, they are addressed in Decision 6. Please note that after factoring in taxation, fees, and inflation effects, the return will be lower than what is presented in this book's examples.

INVESTING YOUNG EXAMPLES

So why is it so essential to invest young? Because *your biggest gains come from your earliest years.* While becoming a millionaire may be a long-term process that requires discipline, the following scenarios show why investing young is so important and how bright the light is at the end of the tunnel.

---

10.   Butler, Dave. "Historical S&P 500 Returns." TheStreet, April 29, 2020. https://www.thestreet.com/investing/annual-sp-500-returns-in-history.

Scenario 1: Investing $300 a Month at Thirty

Meet Kate. Kate graduated from college and spent her twenties like many others: traveling, paying off her student loans, eating out, going to bars, buying new furniture for her apartment, and regularly shopping online. Kate is a dumba$$. Not because she is having fun and enjoying life, but because she is having fun, enjoying life, and *not investing* in her future and therefore wasting her most valuable investing years. Kate is busy spending her twenties investing in other people's futures by buying stuff and making others rich instead of herself. She

never "pays herself first." At age thirty, she has no savings, no personal investments, and a little money in her employer's 401K retirement plan but has made little progress towards being a millionaire. The "stuff" that she spent tens of thousands of dollars on throughout her twenties is mostly unwanted by age thirty. That $3,000 couch she bought at twenty-three is now outdated and has several large stains on it. Sure, she has great memories, but *memories don't make you a millionaire,* and neither do $3,000 couches. By thirty, Kate gets tired of the bar scene and wants to start investing, so she receives this book as a present on her birthday. She reads it and begins investing $300 a month or $3,600 annually in an S&P 500 Index Fund. Starting at thirty and continuing to invest $300 a month, how much is her account worth at sixty?

Scenario	Total Investment	Account Value at 60	Investment Difference	Value Difference
$300/Month from 30-60	$108,000	$ 440,445		

Table 3. Kate's Investment of $300 a Month from Age Thirty to Sixty

By investing $300 a month or $108,000 from age thirty to sixty, Kate's projected account value is $440,445, or roughly four times more than her total contributions. Not bad, but nowhere near being a millionaire.

Scenario 2: Investing $300 a Month at Twenty-Three

Let's now imagine that instead of waiting until thirty, Kate graduates from college at twenty-two. For her college graduation present, Kate's grandparents buy her this book. After reading it and understanding the power of investing young, Kate now invests $300 a month from twenty-three to sixty. By starting seven years earlier and continuing the same strategy as Scenario 1, what is her account value at sixty, and how does it compare to the previous scenario, when she started at thirty?

Scenario	Total Investment	Account Value at 60	Investment Difference	Value Difference
$300/Month from 30-60	$108,000	$440,445		
$300/Month from 23-60	$133,200	$789,537	+$25,200	+$349,092

Table 4. Kate's Investment of $300 a Month Starting at Twenty-Three

Kate's account value is now $789,537, roughly six times more than her total contributions at sixty. By investing $300 a month seven years earlier, or an additional $25,200 from what was invested in Scenario 1, her account value is $349,092.28 more or nearly double that of *starting at thirty*. Getting better, Kate!

Scenario 3: Investing After High School Graduation and During College

For Scenario 3, let's imagine that Kate reads this book during her senior year in high school and becomes extremely motivated to be a millionaire. Kate invests $2,500 from her summer job after high school graduation and $2,500 a year while working part-time during her four years in college, for a total of $12,500. Then she continues the same investment strategy as Scenario 2. What is her account value at sixty, and how does it compare to the previous example, when she started at twenty-three?

IMPORTANT!

Your biggest returns come from your youngest years.

Scenario	Total Investment	Account Value at 60	Investment Difference	Value Difference
$300/Month from 30-60	$108,000	$440,445		
$300/Month from 23-60	$133,200	$789,537		
Investing after High School/ During College to 60	**$145,700**	**$ 1,062,705**	**+$12,500**	**+$273,167.65**

Table 5. Kate's Investment of $300 a Month after High School and During College

Kate's account value is now $1,062,705.05 or 7.3 times her total contributions at age sixty. Just like that, *Kate is a millionaire.* By investing *an additional $12,500* from what was invested in Scenario 2 while working the summer after high school graduation and during all four years in college, her investments earn *another $273,167.65.* Kate's secret? She began investing five years earlier.

Scenario 4: Investing $150 a Month at Sixteen

Finally, let's imagine that at age sixteen, Kate buys her first car and needs $300 a month to pay for her car payment, gas, and insurance.

She gets a job at a local Chick-Fil-A, where she works sixteen hours a week, earning $14 an hour or $224 each week. Kate's paycheck is $350 every two weeks or $700 a month after taxes are withheld. In addition to her car payment, she also decides to put $150 a month into her S&P 500 Index Fund until high school graduation and continues the same investment strategy as described in Scenario 3. By starting three years earlier, what is her account value at sixty, and how does it compare to the previous example, when she started after high school graduation?

Scenario	Total Investment	Account Value at 60	Investment Difference	Value Difference
$300/Month from 30-60	$108,000	$440,445		
$300/Month from 23-60	$133,200	$789,537		
Investing after High School/ During College to 60	$145,700	$1,062,705		
Investing $150/ Month at 16 and Scenario 3	**$151,100**	**$1,210,777**	**+$5,400**	**+$148,072**

Table 6. Kate's Investment of $150 a Month at Starting at Sixteen

Kate's account value is now $1,210,777, or eight times her total contributions at age sixty. By investing *an additional $5,400* during high school, she earns *another $148,072,* or 27.4 times more than the $5,400 investment that she put in. As this scenario shows, Kate gets the most return on the money she invested in high school—her youngest years.

Let's now take a step back and review Scenario 4, when Kate started investing at sixteen while working at Chick-Fil-A and continued until she was sixty. During this exercise, we'll take a closer look and examine each scenario's investment percentage of her $151,100 total investment made from age sixteen to sixty and what percent each scenario accounted for of the total value of $1,210,777.

	Percent of Total Investment ($151,100)	Percent of Total Investment ($1,210,777) at Age 60
Investing $300/Month from 30-60	71.4%	36.4%
Investing $300/Month from 23-30	16.7%	28.8%
Investing after High School and During College to 23	8.3%	22.6%
Investing $150/Month from 16 to High School Graduation	3.6%	12.2%
Total	100%	100%

Table 7. Total Investment Percentage and Total Value for Each of Kate's Scenarios

As the table shows, Kate invested 88.1% of her total investment money in Scenarios 1 and 2 or after college, and it accounted for 65.2% of her account's value at age sixty. Meanwhile, Kate invested 11.9% of her total investment money in Scenarios 3 and 4 while working part-time in high school and college, which accounted for 34.8% of her account's investment value at age sixty. In addition, money invested before thirty accounted for 28.6% of the total investment money but 63.6% of her account's value at age sixty. This is an extremely important concept to remember because this chart highlights why investments made in your teens and early twenties are so *valuable because investments made in your youngest years will be the most valuable and make up a large percentage of your total gains later in life.*

Many of you reading this book may be in high school or college, and it's important to remember this example when deciding what to do with your part-time high school or college paychecks. Remember, *money is money no matter what, and investments made before your "real job" make up a larger percentage of your future net worth.* We aren't trying to get preachy, but if you are working in high school or college and not investing some of your paycheck, you are missing out on a tremendous opportunity to make a lot of money later in life.

What do these scenarios prove? They emphasize three important points: one, the importance of *investing young*. Kate invested at a younger age in each scenario, which resulted in significantly more money; *time was more important than the amount.* Two, being a millionaire comes down to smart life choices. *Kate always chose to pay herself first.* Kate chose to invest young. Three, Kate's job had no impact on her being a millionaire. What mattered was that she had a job and was investing money. There is no need to wait for your "real job" as long as you invest. Each of you can make the same choices. You can choose to go out two instead of three nights a week. You can choose to start investing in your teens and twenties instead of your thirties. You can choose to be a millionaire. As these scenarios show, it doesn't take a whole lot of money to be a millionaire. In Kate's example, *time turned $151,100 into $1,210,777* because she *chose* to invest young.

> **NOTE TO SELF**
>
> " It doesn't take a lot to be a millionaire. Investing young turned $151,100 into $1,210,777. "

We know what some of you may be thinking. "I'm only young once. I want to experience life and wait until I get my 'real job' before investing." In terms of life experience, you may have a point; however, you couldn't be more wrong financially. What if Kate waited until thirty-five or even forty to begin investing $300 a month, and how does it compare to the previous scenarios?

Starting Age	Total Investment	Account Value at 60
23 (Scenario 2)	$133,200	$789,537
30 (Scenario 1)	$108,000	$440,445
35	$90,000	$284,235
40	$72,000	$179,923

Table 8. Kate's Investment of $300 a Month Starting at Different Ages

As we just showed, waiting to invest until your thirties or later puts you at a significant disadvantage. But how much more money is needed to be a millionaire if you delay investing for "another time?" Let's take a look.

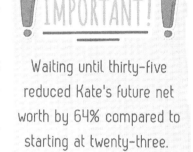

Did you know that investing $529.32 a month from your twentieth to thirtieth birthday will be worth a million dollars on your sixtieth birthday assuming an 8% annual return? Assuming the same return, how much

Waiting until thirty-five reduced Kate's future net worth by 64% compared to starting at twenty-three.

would you have to invest each month if you wanted to be a millionaire on your sixtieth birthday if you only invested in your thirties? Only in your forties? And only in your fifties?

Age	Monthly Investment Needed to Become a Millionaire at 60	Total Investment Needed to Become a Millionaire at 60
20s Only	$529.32	$63,518.40
30s Only	$1,138.04	$136,564.80
40s Only	$2,446.78	$293,613.60
50s Only	$5,260.58	$631,269.60

Table 9. Monthly Investment Amount Required to Become a Millionaire at Sixty

Table 9 shows that the *younger you invest, the less money you need to become a millionaire.* Conversely, *the longer you wait to invest, the more money you will need to become a millionaire.* To be a millionaire, you must do your "investing time." In other words, you delay some level of instant gratification and invest to become a millionaire. The question then becomes, *why not be efficient and take the route that requires the least amount of money?* Why not put aside $63,518 instead of $293,614 to become a millionaire? *Investing as young as possible is when the odds are in your favor, and you get the most bang for your buck.* Investing young is so important and *has to be part the central piece or focal point of your strategy.*

Table 9 also proves that you can still become a millionaire if you don't invest young and instead start later in life; however, *investing more... a lot more... is the only way to make up for lost time.* In this example, you need to invest roughly 2.1 times more a month in your thirties, approximately 4.6 times more in your forties, and about 9.9 times more in your fifties than what you had to invest in your twenties. Time is money!

"I DON'T WANT TO WAIT UNTIL I'M SIXTY TO BE A MILLIONAIRE"

Some of you might be reading the examples above and thinking, "I don't want to wait until I'm sixty to be a millionaire." You might also be discouraged from waiting forty years to accomplish your goal, and you have every right to be frustrated. This book applies simple investing concepts to easy-to-understand situations to easily communicate the point to the reader. However, other variables are not detailed in this chapter or book that significantly reduce the time it takes to become a millionaire. Some include *getting married, investing more each month than the examples in this book,* and *owning a home/real estate.*

First, getting married helps because together, there are *two incomes but only one living expense* if both work. The financial benefits of being married are powerful. For example, instead of investing $300, $400, or $500 a month when you're not married, you may be able to invest $1,500, $1,800, or $2,000 a month when married if both work, which dramatically cuts down on how long it takes to become a millionaire.

Second, even if you're not married, you may be able to afford more than the $300 a month we used in many examples. Everyone is different, and some may have an easier time not spending money than others or earn a higher salary which allows more than $300. Also, our example assumed Kate invested $300 a month and never increased her monthly investment over roughly forty years. This would have meant she never earned a promotion or had a pay raise, which is highly unlikely. In reality, as Kate gets older and gains more work experience, she makes more money and invests more, which cuts down on the time it takes to become a millionaire.

Third and final, we did not discuss owning a home or real estate. Real estate equity, or how much ownership is yours, can also be counted towards your million dollars. Living expenses such as rent or a mortgage are likely your highest monthly expense, and by owning a home instead of renting, *you turn your highest expense into your highest investment*. Renting an apartment or house and leasing a car are similar: You pay money to use it but when your contract is up, you have nothing. Instead of paying rent and making *your landlord* rich, you are paying your mortgage and making *yourself* rich. Over time, you will build real estate equity that adds to your total net worth. For example, we bought and sold two different houses within the first ten years after college and made a high return on both. We then invested the proceeds in the stock market, which helped accelerate our journey to becoming a millionaire. If we had never bought a house and instead rented the entire time, we would have thrown a lot of money away, and our net worth would be much less than it is today.

While doing any of the three options above decreases the time it takes to become a millionaire, doing all three together significantly cuts down the time. What made us millionaires at thirty-three is doing all three.

DO I REALLY HAVE TO INVEST UNTIL I'M SIXTY?

Think of investing and making money like growing a tree. Growing a tall tree, like becoming a millionaire, requires time. When starting out, a young tree requires care, such as adequate water and nutrients, to help it get established. Likewise, a young investment needs care, such as additional investments. At some point, the tree becomes self-sufficient, and additional assistance provides minimal improvement. The same concept can be applied to investing. First, plant your tree "seed" by opening an account and investing. Then, give it "water and nutrients" by regularly investing. Like a tree, your investment eventually becomes self-sufficient. Eventually, an investment's daily market fluctuations exceed monthly contributions. At this point, an investment's size becomes like an ocean, and monthly contributions are equivalent to adding a few drops of water. The ocean, or an investment's size, is so large that adding a few drops of water, or monthly contributions, has little impact on changing the size of the ocean.

So far, the examples in this book have shown how much money could be made if someone started at a certain age and continued until sixty. If money is set aside and invested in the present, it is expected to be worth it. However, there comes a point in time when investing doesn't make as much sense since investment length or time is limited.

For example, let's reexamine Kate's Scenario 2, where she had $789,537 at age sixty by investing $300 a month from twenty-three to sixty. Of course, not all of Kate's contributions are equal; some are "worth more" than others. For example, her $3,600 investment made at age twenty-three has a future net value of $62,084 or roughly 7.8% of the total investment value at age sixty.

Meanwhile, her $3,600 investment made at age fifty-nine has a future net value of $3,888, or roughly 0.5% of the total investment value at age sixty. Clearly, there's not as much bang for the buck on Kate's investment money in her later years. So, as time goes on, investments of the same amount lose their effectiveness because the return is lower due to less investment time.

With all this in mind, what if Kate ONLY invests from age twenty-three until her fortieth birthday or seventeen years total? How does it compare to investing until she's sixty or thirty-seven years total?

Scenario	Total Investment	Account Value at 60	Investment Difference	Value Difference
$300/Month from 23-60	$133,200	$789,537	+$72,000	+$128,993
$300/Month from 23-40	$61,200	$660,544		

Table 10. Kate's Investment of $300 a Month from Twenty-Three to Sixty Compared to Twenty-Three to Forty

If Kate stopped investing on her fortieth birthday, she would have roughly 17% or $128,993 less compared to investing for another twenty years. More importantly, Kate invested less money to make more. *Kate's* *first $61,200 investment made her $660,544 or a 1,079% return, while the last $72,000 investment only made her an additional $128,993 or a 179% return.* By planting her tree at twenty-three, Kate continued providing nutrients until forty. Her tree was mostly self-sufficient at that point.

$789,537

$660,544

Investing $300/Month from 23-60

Investing $300/Month from 23-40

This scenario highlights why we won't invest past our fortieth birthday unless there is a significant stock market correction. The upside is limited and less attractive than in our twenties and thirties. We spent our twenties and thirties aggressively saving and investing as much as possible to grow our tree as big and fast as possible. Starting at forty, we plan on spending our "what would be" investing money on nice cars, houses, vacations, and other things that we suggest twenty and thirty-year-olds avoid if they want to become millionaires. We aren't bragging but are trying to prove an important point. We can do this because *our tree was planted in our early twenties and received a substantial amount of nutrients by continually investing.* By forty, our tree will be self-sufficient, and we can then afford to be less money-conscious instead of applying additional nutrients. Therefore, money invested from forty onward has a limited impact on its size.

So, back to the original question, "Do you really need to invest until you're sixty?" No, because most of your gains will be from what is invested in your twenties and thirties and investing later has minimal upside.

OPERATION DON'T BE A DUMBA$$
Your Mission:
Plant your tree as early as possible.

FORECASTING FUTURE NET WORTH—THE ONLY MATH THAT REALLY MATTERS AND MOTIVATES

At this point, many of you may be asking yourselves, "How did you forecast how much money Kate was going to have at age sixty?", or, "How did you know how much money Kate would have if she only invested from twenty-three to forty?" Let's quickly discuss the only math equation in this book: forecasting future net worth or projecting how much you should have in the future.

> "
> The goal of forecasting is not to predict the future, but to tell you what you need to know to take meaningful action in the present.
> –Paul Saffo
> "

Forecasting future net worth is important for two reasons. First, it provides visibility into your financial future and makes it tangible today. Second, it serves as a motivator to adhere to your budget. Forecasting future net worth helps justify spending limits today for a better tomorrow. For example, if saving $250 a month by cutting back on your lifestyle results in hundreds of thousands of dollars later in life, not going to Starbucks every day. Thus, being able to "see" your future net worth on a spreadsheet or app makes it seem "real."

Ultimately being driven to own Buffalo County hunting land, Adam's forecasting and going through "what if" scenarios on his future net worth spreadsheets helped him stay focused for many years. While in his twenties, Adam would regularly investigate the impact a lifestyle change here and there would have on his financial future. He quickly realized that a $50 or $100 additional investment had a tremendous impact on his future. As a result, he believes forecasting inspires and keeps young investors motivated and focused on the goal.

There are apps that calculate future net worth, but Adam has always used Microsoft Excel, which is an excellent tool for forecasting wealth as it allows the user to interact and modify current inputs. Since investments are made over many years, Excel provides a holistic view. If you are interested in learning how to use Microsoft Excel for forecasting, please watch forecasting demos on YouTube. Also, consider researching on investor.gov, which has a lot of great information.

Overall, if you retain one thing from this chapter, it is this: *Always pay yourself first by investing as much and as early as possible,* even if it's as little as $50 a month. Because as this chapter demonstrates, time turns a little money into A LOT of money. Start somewhere. While your initial amount may not be as high as examples in this book, *the discipline to pay yourself first and not spend all your money at a young age is most valuable.* It's important to train yourself that your paycheck is not what shows up in your checking account but

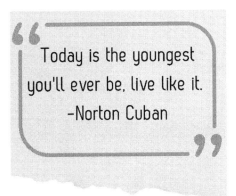

Today is the youngest you'll ever be, live like it.
—Norton Cuban

FUTURE NET WORTH
CALCULATIONS

To calculate future net worth, use the following formula:
Future Value = Investment Amount x (1+Annual return
Expressed as Decimal)$^{\text{Years Invested}}$

Or also shown as
$$A=P(1+r)^t$$

where *P* is the investment amount, *r* is annual return
as a decimal and *t* is time (usually displayed in years).
What's important is Future Value is a function of t or
time to the *exponential power*. So, as Kate demonstrated
in this chapter, the longer money is invested, the more it
will be worth.

For example, how much would $10,000 be worth in 25
years with an 8% annual return?
Future Value = $10,000 x (1 +0.08)^{25}
or $10,000 x (1.08)^{25} = $68,484.75

HOW DID WE CALCULATE HOW MUCH INVESTING $300/MONTH IS WORTH AT AGE 60 STARTING AT AGE 23?

Future Value of Annual Investments Made from ages 23 to 59

Age 23: $3,600 x $(1.08)^{(60-23)}$ = $62,084
Age 24: $3,600 x $(1.08)^{(60-24)}$ = $57,485
Age 25: $3,600 x $(1.08)^{(60-25)}$ = $53,227

$$\vdots$$

Age 30: $3,600 x $(1.08)^{(60-30)}$ = $36,226

$$\vdots$$

Age 40: $3,600 x $(1.08)^{(60-40)}$ = $16,779

$$\vdots$$

Age 59: $3,600 x $(1.08)^{(60-59)}$ = $3,888

Total (Age 60) $789,537

The total future value at age 60 is then calculated by adding up all the individual year's future value from ages 23 to 59 together or in this example, $789,537.

rather *how much is left after subtracting your investing money*. As you get older and obtain more work experience, your income will go up. At that point, the habit of paying yourself first by investing will become second nature, and you will most likely be able to invest a lot more than you did in your teens and twenties. This chapter's charts, scenarios, and personal stories show that investing takes time, patience, discipline, and knowledge. The forecasted net worth is your light at the end of the tunnel and is the evidence and motivation you need to start investing young.

Not everyone can be a doctor, celebrity, or professional athlete, but that does not mean you cannot be a millionaire. Teachers, law enforcement, military personnel, plumbers, and dental hygienists can all be millionaires by paying themselves first and, most importantly, investing young. Investing at seventeen is better than twenty-one. Investing at twenty-three is better than twenty-five. Investing at twenty-five is better than thirty and so forth. For the final time, *the age at which you start investing has the most profound impact on your wealth*. It is that simple. There is no secret formula.

A friend of ours once said, "Life is not fair because when you are young, you have no money but a lot of time, and when you are old, you have a lot of money but no time." In other words, those who choose to be different and invest young when they are earning less money compared to when they earn a higher income are destined to be millionaires. Today, you are the youngest you'll ever be. Of course, there is something to be said about immediate versus long-term satisfaction. There is a need to have balance when it comes to your finances. The important point is to recognize they both play a hand in successful finances. You cannot just focus on one versus the other. Excluding a once-in-a-lifetime pandemic, you can travel to Europe, go on a cruise, or go to concerts at any point in your life; however, you can only invest while you are young *once.*

Before we conclude, let's revisit the question proposed at the beginning of the chapter: Would you rather have $900,000 or what $10,000 would be worth in sixty years with an 8% return? Did Kate possibly change your answer? As was pointed out in this chapter, a lot of time can turn a small amount of money into a lot of money. In this scenario, $10,000 is worth $1,012,571 after being invested for sixty years with an 8% annual return. Hopefully, you are now beginning to see the future value in money and not always take the immediate thing, whether it's a vacation, a new car, or even $900,000.

KEY TAKEAWAYS OF DECISION 2

- Time is your most powerful weapon
- The earlier you begin investing, the easier it will be to become a millionaire
- Always pay yourself first and make yourself rich

DECISION 3: CREATE A BUDGET AND STICK TO IT

"Budgeting isn't about limiting yourself. It's about making the things that excite you possible."
-Unknown

"My first Air Force assignment was at Nellis Air Force Base (shout out to the 59th and 422nd) in Las Vegas. I was fresh out of college and earning my first 'real job' paycheck. I thought I had partied hard and seen it all at the University of Wisconsin, but Vegas takes temptation and partying to a whole new level. Gambling, shows, world-renowned restaurants, girls, drinking, drugs, nightclubs. You name it, Vegas has it, and it is easily accessible. Every. Single. Day. And it is because of these reasons Vegas is known as 'Sin City.'

Shortly after arriving in Vegas, I attended an Air Force welcoming brief to review what to expect from the city. The speaker started the brief by saying, 'To all the men in the room, I'm going to let you in on a little secret. You are NOT good-looking. I don't care what you are told, but you are NOT good-looking!' We all looked around the room at each other, puzzled why he started his presentation by talking about men's looks. However, he eventually gets to the point that in Vegas, prostitution was an issue and usually began with an oblivious man being approached and complimented by a woman. This could easily be a point where any visitor or recent arrival could get himself in a lot of trouble. Unfortunately, other service members had gotten in trouble with it in the past, and he was warning us to be aware of what was out there.

What does a story about Vegas, prostitution, and being in the Air Force have to do with a chapter about **budgeting**? Because *regardless of where you are in life, you will always be tempted to do things that detract from your budget. No matter your age, there will always be peer pressure and temptations. The car you've always wanted is on sale for a limited time. Your friends want to go to Nashville for a long weekend. Consistently **sticking to your budget is hard. It's damn hard**. But, to be successful, it's important to ignore peer pressure, temptation, and instant gratification. Sometimes you may have to decline because you can't afford to go or buy something no matter how much you want it. A budget doesn't allow for 'one-time' exceptions unless it's an emergency.*

*Being exposed to the temptations that Vegas offers could have easily put me over the edge and got me in trouble, both financially and non-financially. I'll be honest. I still had fun and made a lot of great memories. But **I was smart about it**. I never compromised my morals and rarely compromised my long-term financial goals for short-term satisfaction. Maybe I didn't party with big-name celebrities or split a $5,000 nightclub table with some friends, but at the end of the day, who gives a shit about things like that? I certainly don't. In fifteen years, what's more important...telling someone a ten-minute story about all the crazy nights you had in Vegas or having a million dollars?" –Adam*

So far, you have learned the importance of goal-setting and investing young and are now motivated to get started. Recall from the introduction, becoming a millionaire is a straightforward strategy that is a function of three inputs: *when you start, how much you invest, and what you invest in*. These elements are *in your control*, and *only you can make it happen*. The second input, how much you invest, directly relates to how much money you have available, which correlates to proper money management through budgeting, the next decision.

Whether you are working part-time for extra money in high school or college or have a full-time job, you need a budget. It is your financial roadmap and gives *visibility to where your money goes*. Budgeting is like using a map because it is difficult to reach your destination (financial goals) without one. From there, *it's your job to memorize it, adhere to it,*

> **NOTE TO SELF**
> " A budget is your financial road map, so you can see where you are going. "

and at all times, reevaluate it so you can cut any unnecessary expenses to free up additional money to invest. A sturdy financial house requires a solid foundation, and a budget is that foundation. So this chapter's main takeaway is: If you don't want to be a dumba$$, **make a budget and stick to it**.

First, a budget must be *realistic or something you can adhere to*. Overall, it is difficult to achieve your long-term financial goals without a budget, your roadmap. As the old saying goes, "If you don't know where you are going, you'll end up somewhere else." Rephrasing this financially, "If you don't know where your money goes, you'll end up broke."

To create a budget, follow these six steps:

Step 1: Calculate or estimate your monthly take-home pay. Write it down.

Step 2: Input your monthly investment income. The first expense in your budget should be investing money. Starting your budget this way ensures you have investment money, makes investing your top priority, and *forces you to cut down on other expenses rather than making your investments fit into your budget.*

Step 3: Create a monthly mandatory expense list. These are expenses that must be paid every month to survive. Some mandatory expenses include student loan payments, cell phone bills, rent or mortgage, car expenses (monthly payment, insurance, and gas), utilities, and groceries. Next, write down whether the expense is due the first (1st–14th) or second (15th–end) half of each month. If you earn more than one paycheck a month, align the expense's due date with the corresponding pay period. For example, a $100 cell phone bill due on the fifth of every month should be placed in the first half of the month's budget since it falls between the first and fifteenth of the month.

> " Do not save what is left after spending, but spend what is left after saving.
> –Warren Buffet "

Step 4: Calculate your monthly fun or spending money. Fun or spending money is anything that is not mandatory to live, including eating out, coffee, movies, bars, clothes, online purchases, and vacations.

NOTE TO SELF

" If you don't know where your money is going, you will end up broke. "

Step 5: Place your budget with your income and expenses somewhere it can be viewed daily, such as on a refrigerator or bathroom mirror. Viewing it regularly reinforces the numbers and helps engrain the discipline needed to adhere to it. You can also download budget apps on your Smartphone to help track your spending. Popular apps include You Need a Budget, Mint, PocketGuard, and Expensify.

Step 6: Track it and make adjustments as required. It is highly unlikely that your first budget will be perfect, and it will most likely take several iterations until you figure out what works for you. If adjustments are needed, it's important to adjust non-investment money because, under most circumstances, you can't become a millionaire if you don't invest.

A BUDGETING EXAMPLE

Let's apply the concepts discussed to a budgeting example. Below is a sample monthly spreadsheet for John, twenty-three, who recently graduated from college. John's take-home paycheck or income is $2,000 every two weeks, and he is paid on the first and fifteenth of the month. Using concepts from this chapter, the first thing he does is budget $300 a month for investments during the first half of the month. Then, after making investing his top budget priority, John fills out his other monthly expenses on his budget, Table 11. Everything listed on the left side shows John's financial activity during the first half of the month, while everything on the right side lists John's financial activity during the second half of the month.

John's income, or $2,000, is shown on the top line for both pay periods because that's how much he earns. Meanwhile, all his expenses are listed under "Expenses." John's total expenses are then subtracted from his income. John's remaining balance is on the bottom next to "Remaining Funds."

NOTE TO SELF

" Your budget should be visible at all times as a constant reminder. Putting it in your sock drawer won't cut it. "

For the month, John makes $4,000, and his expenses are $4,900 ($3,850 during the first half of the month and $1,050 during the second half of the month). In other words, *John has a $900 monthly deficit* or *spends $900 more each month than he earns.* Something has to be done because having a $900 monthly deficit is not financially sustainable.

First Half of the Month		Second Half of the Month	
Paycheck	$ 2,000.00	Paycheck	$2,000.00
Expenses		Expenses	
S&P500 Index Investment	$ 300.00	Groceries	$ 200.00
Rent	$ 1,000.00	Gasoline	$ 50.00
Car Payment	$ 400.00	Spending	$ 800.00
Cell Phone	$ 150.00	Total Expenses	$1,050.00
Cable/Internet	$ 75.00		
Utilities (Electric)	$ 125.00		
Utilities (Gas)	$ 50.00		
Gym Membership	$ 100.00		
College Loan Payment	$ 600.00		
Gasoline	$ 50.00		
Groceries	$ 200.00		
Spending	$ 800.00		
Total Expenses	$ 3,850.00		
Remaining Funds	$(1,850.00)	Remaining Funds	$ 950.00
		Monthly Remaining Funds	$ (900.00)

Table 11. John's Budget

At this point, John has three options. Option 1: charge his $900 deficit to his credit card, which he will be charged a high-interest rate, costing him thousands of dollars and possibly eventually making him go bankrupt due to high credit card debt. Option 2: make more money or income, whether it is a pay raise or a second source of income. Option 3: cut expenses by changing his lifestyle.

The critical takeaway from John's budget is that a spreadsheet provides *clear visibility of his finances,* allowing him to visually know and understand where his money is going. If John has issues, his budget allows him to identify and resolve them. However, we have not seen the end of John because in *Decision 5: Buy Needs Instead of Wants*, we will revisit his budget situation.

HELP! I WENT OVER BUDGET LAST MONTH; WHAT SHOULD I DO NOW?

Life is unpredictable and throws curveballs. And when it happens, it is important to stay diligent. There will be pay periods when you spend less than your budget, which is great. However, you will also have periods when spending exceeds your budget. Holiday shopping, vacations, visitors, special events, and unforeseen expenses such as car repairs and medical emergencies do happen and will blow up your budget.

OPERATION DON'T BE A DUMBA$$

Your Mission:
Create a budget and
stick to it.

When this happens, commit to preemptive or post-spending cuts. Spending less before or after is necessary to offset the excess spending and help balance your budget. For example, let's say you budget $800 for fun money every two weeks. At the end of the month, you have family visiting. You expect their visit will cost an additional $400, and project your fun money will be $1,200. To offset the projected $400 in additional fun money, you can either cut back beforehand, cut back after they visit, or a combination of both. The critical lesson of budgeting is it provides visibility, eliminates financial surprises, and allows you to make necessary adjustments.

Excessive spending is a slippery slope, and if not careful, anyone can easily fall behind, carry an outstanding credit card balance, and pay high credit card fees. It can even lead to bankruptcy. Budgeting requires you to manage your money actively and avoid that slope. Budgeting is a lot like playing a sport. Life, similar to an opponent in sports, is unknown and requires your constant attention and adjustment to be successful. Thus, *budgeting is a contact sport, and regular interaction and adjustments are needed.*

NOTE TO SELF

"Budgeting is a contact sport, and regular interaction is necessary to be successful."

CREDIT CARDS: THE MONSTERS UNDER YOUR FINANCIAL BED

Lastly, let's address credit cards and the financial dangers they can impose. Just to cover our basis, a bank or credit card company issues credit cards to individuals and allows the credit card owner to make purchases on credit in agreement that the balance is paid back. Many credit cards offer credit as high as $5,000 or more. The seduction of buying something you want today only to pay for it later is attractive. However, some forget that *everything bought has to be paid back* and this is where people get in trouble. We live in a society of instant gratification, which is why credit cards can be financially dangerous. That beautiful, shiny piece of plastic that can buy you nearly anything you want can quickly turn into financial poison and ruin your future if not used properly. According to Experian's annual Consumer Credit

Review, the average credit card balance per household in the United States in 2019 was $6,194, which shows how prevalent credit card debt is among Americans.[11]

How quickly can credit card debt ruin your financial future? Let's say that shortly after your eighteenth birthday, you apply and receive your first credit card. Finally, you have the financial freedom that you've always wanted. You no longer have to pay cash but can buy more stuff than you can normally afford because you have the freedom to pay it back "later." So you go to the mall and purchase $800 worth of clothes and a $1,200 TV at Best Buy, you begin to eat out more, and then you buy the nice shoes to match your new clothes. "This is great," you tell yourself. "I can now afford to buy things that I've always wanted." However, at the end of the month you receive your credit card statement, and you owe $3,000. $3,000!?! How are you going to pay that off? You have a part-time job and earn about $300 every two weeks. Now what happens?

NOTE TO SELF
You choose to spend or to not spend your money.

If your credit card balance is more than what you can afford to pay off, high fees (15% interest or higher) are charged to your balance, resulting in you paying substantially more than you had originally charged. These high fees may likely take years to pay off, significantly affecting your budget. On the contrary, credit cards can be a great asset if used responsibly; many offer good reward programs such as cashback, hotel stays, or airline miles. Proper credit card use also builds your

11.   Amadeo, Kimberly. "Average U.S. Credit Card Debt Statistics." The Balance, November 29, 2021. https://www.thebalance.com/averagecredit-card-debt-u-s-statistics-3305919.

credit score when payments are paid in a timely manner. A high credit score is important when taking out loans. A higher score can lower its loan interest rate, reducing your monthly loan payment. Overall, credit cards have their place in everyone's wallet or purse but should be used responsibly.

HOW TO AVOID CREDIT CARD DEBT

Credit card debt can only be avoided by using one simple rule: *only charge what can be fully paid at the end of the month unless it is an absolute emergency.* It is that simple. Your budget will tell you how much can be charged monthly and is the reason why your budget or financial visibility tool is so critical. It helps you steer clear of credit card debt or financial poison. What helped *us* successfully control our credit card spending? We use our credit cards as if they're debit cards—cards that automatically deduct from a checking account and require adequate funds in that account to cover the charge. If we don't have money in our account to pay off the balance at the end of the month, we don't charge the credit card.

FAKE NEWS

A shoe sale counts as an emergency

For example, our budget allows us to charge $1,980 during the first half of the month. If the credit card balance reaches $1,980 BEFORE the end of the first half of the month, *we stop spending.* It's as simple and straightforward as that. We don't buy anything until the next pay period, and our spending amount is reset. If that means eating eggs and toast for dinner for four nights until we get paid again, then that's what we do. Because of our budget, we know how much can be charged to our credit card, actively track every credit card charge, and know how much we have left to spend. We regularly ask each other, "How much is on the credit card?" before making purchases to help stay on budget. If we have surplus spending money at the end of the month, we either invest it or put it in our vacation fund.

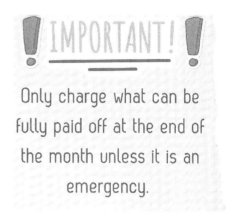

Only charge what can be fully paid off at the end of the month unless it is an emergency.

What is the lesson here? Always know your charging limit (mandatory expenses charged to your credit card and fun money) for each pay period, track your charges daily, and *stop charging once the balance reaches your spending limit* unless it is an absolute emergency (which should be rare).

Lastly, let's talk about credit card emergency charges. As we said, *we only charge what can be fully paid off at the end of the month unless it's an emergency*. When we say "an emergency," we are not talking about a big sale. We mean rare, unforeseen issues that must be addressed, like car problems, medical emergencies, or family emergencies. Consistently stay firm on what constitutes "an emergency," and if you have an emergency, be sure to cut back on spending until enough surplus covers your emergency expenses.

A BAD IDEA: PAYING OFF YOUR CREDIT CARD BALANCE WITH THE MINIMUM PAYMENT

Have you ever wondered why credit card companies make so much money? One reason is that some customers, who have poor money management habits or don't know any better, pay the credit card company's high fees on late payments. To "help" their financially illiterate customers, credit card

FAKE NEWS

Making the minimum payment is an affordable way to pay off your credit card.

companies offer an "affordable" minimum payment. Who wouldn't want to pay off a $5,000 credit card bill with a $45 monthly payment? "My budget can afford a $45 monthly credit card payment!" you may tell yourself. However, many customers are unaware that a high-interest rate is included and disguised in that "affordable" minimum payment. The appeal of making a small payment on a large credit balance is enticing. Who wouldn't want to buy a $2,000 TV and only pay $15 a month for it? But ask yourself, is it really a minimum payment, and who does it benefit? A credit card's minimum payment is generally calculated by taking 1 to 3% of the outstanding balance and adding late fees and interest.[12] In reality, these high-interest rates are disguised as low monthly payments.

So, just how much do you pay by making minimum payments? Table 12 shows how long and how much a typical credit card user pays by making 3% minimum payments with a 20.2% interest rate.[13]

---

12.   Tsosie, Claire. "How Credit Card Issuers Calculate Minimum Payments." NerdWallet, March 24, 2022. https://www.nerdwallet.com/article/credit-cards/credit-card-issuer-minimum-payment.
13.   Ibid.

Credit Card Balance	Payment Duration	Total Interest Paid	Total Amount Paid	Interest to Balance Percentage
$5,000	18 years, 7 months	$5,993.22	$10,993.22	119.9%
$10,000	22 years, 11 months	$12,395.67	$22,395.67	124.0%
$15,000	25 years, 5 months	$18,778.07	$33,778.07	125.2%
$25,000	28 years, 8 months	$31,562.75	$56,562.75	126.3%

Table 12. Credit Card Minimum Payment Chart Calculated With Bankrate Calculator [14]

Paying the credit card's minimum balance *results in the credit holder paying more than twice what the original credit card charges were and can take over twenty years to pay it off.* Let's say you are nineteen years old and you charge $5,000 for clothes, a flat-screen TV, and other purchases and decide to pay by making the minimum payments. By

NOTE TO SELF

66 Paying a credit card's minimum payment could result in paying double for all your purchases. 99

doing so, *you will be thirty-seven when the balance is paid off.* Whatever was bought at age nineteen is most likely in the trash by thirty-seven, yet you are still paying for it. The $2,000 TV ended up costing $4,000. *You are making the credit card companies richer by paying high-interest rates and making yourself poorer.* In this instance, twice as poor. Paying more for your purchases results in less investment money, which decreases your long-term financial future. Not only are you investing less, but any additional credit card charges will further delay the final payoff date, causing a potential inescapable pattern. Improperly using

14.   "Minimum Payment Calculator." Bankrate, accessed April 5, 2021. https://www.bankrate.com/finance/credit-cards/minimum-payment-calculator/.

credit cards can create inescapable financial holes, making people feel hopeless. What is the lesson here? *The first rule of credit card debt is to always use them responsibly and not get into credit card debt.* Unless it is an emergency, do not put anything on a credit card that you can't pay for at the end of the pay period. *Careless credit card spending is a 100% guaranteed way to destroy your financial future.*

HOW TO PLAN FOR THE UNEXPECTED: CREATE AND SAVE AN EMERGENCY FUND

Finally, being prepared for when life throws you a curveball is necessary. To be prepared, save and build up an emergency fund that consists of three to six months of your monthly living expenses in an easy, accessible account, such as a savings account, to use during challenging times. Should you experience a temporary setback, use these funds to cover living expenses until you get back on

IMPORTANT!

Careless credit card spending is a guaranteed way to destroy your financial future.

your feet. Once you recover, replenish your emergency fund. Building up your emergency fund will take time. You should not put 100% of any extra income into it because putting all your extra income into an emergency fund takes away from your investing money, which should be a higher priority. After establishing your realistic budget, assess how much you can set aside from each paycheck. Remember, *making good life choices is the central theme of this book; therefore, accounting for the unexpected and being prepared is necessary.*

To conclude, walking through life without a budget is like walking through a dark cave without a flashlight. You will bump into things, fall, and get beat up in that cave. William Feather said, "A budget tells us what we can't afford, but it doesn't keep us from buying it,"[15] which means a budget is only as good as you are willing to adhere to it. You are the only one in charge of your budget and finances. *You choose to spend or not to spend money. Make the right decision.* By **making it your goal to become a millionaire**, **investing young,** and then **creating a budget,** you are on the right path. A budget is your financial road map to show where your money goes. From there, you can then identify and correct poor money management and behavior. Remember, budgeting takes practice. Your first budget will rarely be right and will most likely require several adjustments as you figure out what works for you. Whether a recent high school graduate or a millionaire, everyone needs a budget.

KEY TAKEAWAYS OF DECISION 3:

- Budgeting is your financial guide and necessary to see where your money goes
- Your budget should be realistic
- Post your budget as a visible, regular reminder
- Stick to your budget
- Only charge what you can fully pay off at the end of the month unless it is an emergency
- Budget your investment money first, then expenses around it

---

15.   Feather, William. "A Budget Tells Us What We can't Afford, but It Doesn't Keep Us from Buying It." Forbes Quotes, accessed May 16, 2022. https://www.forbes.com/quotes/9838/.

DECISION 4: CHOOSE A MARKETABLE CAREER

> "I am not a product of my circumstances.
> I am a product of my decisions."
> -Stephen Covey

*"I was the first person in my family to go to college, let alone get a master's degree. As you know by now, my parents taught me many lessons about what not to do in life by being examples of what I didn't want to be like. Going to school and **getting a marketable career** is one of those lessons. As far back as I can remember, my dad never had a nine-to-five job. He is what you could call a hustler. He was always hustling from this job to that job or trying to find his next gig. My dad wanted to be a stand-up comedian his entire life, which is why he moved to Las Vegas when he was young. To be fair, he is actually very funny. He can put a smile on anyone's face just by pointing out the funny complexities of life, BUT he is not funny enough to be the next Dane Cook, Jeff Foxworthy, or Dave Chappelle. He is not funny enough to 'make it.' Or maybe he just wasn't in the right place at the right time. Regardless, here is the thing about making decisions about what to do after high school: Every decision has consequences. By thinking he would make it, my dad never took the time to work **a marketable career to make decent money and have some stability in life.***

So, what happened to him? Today, he is sixty-five years old and still working whatever gig he can find. Right now, he is a car auctioneer. But, he still does not have a guaranteed paycheck to this day. He gets a gig when he gets a gig. He doesn't have the job security to know that his paycheck will be in his bank account every month on the first and fifteenth. He doesn't have a salary, health insurance, retirement benefits—none of it. By being a hustler, he somehow has hustled through every month and made ends meet. But why? Why live life wondering if you will have a gig next weekend and be able to buy food? Why live life wondering if you can pay rent? Some people don't mind living like that. Personally, it is not for me.

*To be clear, I am not saying choose a career you don't want or do something just for the money, but ensure your job or degree is marketable and if you continue education beyond high school, **avoid getting into high levels of debt attaining it**. Does my dad regret chasing his dream? I don't know. But what I do know is this: My dad will work until the day that he dies because he doesn't have the money not to work. Sure, my dad is full of jokes, but sadly at sixty-five with no retirement, renting an apartment, living gig to gig—the joke is on him."* –Heather

At this point, you should understand the importance of goal-setting, investing young, and adhering to a budget. *The next important decision you make is what you do after high school.* Everyone will choose to do something, and it mostly boils down to four major options:

Option 1: Go straight to the workforce

Option 2: Attend a four-year college (public or private)

Option 3: Acquire vocational training (trade school, community college, or apprenticeships)

Option 4: Join the military

Before we dive in, to be clear, we are not for or against one career decision over another. Instead, we are for you to decide your future with your eyes wide open, knowing as much information as possible. But, in the end, everyone needs to do what's right for them.

Choosing a marketable career is important because your job provides the income needed to invest. A marketable career is a career with a high prospectus of employment, advancement, and salary growth and one that won't become obsolete in the future. No or little income = no investment money, which means little chance of becoming a millionaire. Also, the amount of student loan debt that it takes to obtain your career is important. High student loan payments can easily consume a significant amount of your monthly budget, which means little to no investment money after college and more importantly, little to no investment money during your most valuable investment years. Investing young becomes difficult when you have a job with low prospects, low salary, or high student loan payments. Therefore, *deciding what you do after high school and how much it costs to obtain it greatly influences your ability to invest young, which we saw earlier provides the highest probability of becoming a millionaire.* Hopefully by now, you can begin to see how many of these decisions overlap and influence one another, and it will become more apparent as we continue in this book.

As you can imagine, there are countless career possibilities and options that tie back to your earning potential and debt. What type of education will you receive? Will you earn any scholarships? What's the starting salary for your intended career?

SAD FACT:
Many young adults fail to see how student loan payments affect their ability to invest while young.

What are the chances that you can get a job? The point is there is no possible way for us to discuss every variation of your post-high school decisions, but what we can do is show a few common scenarios that you will soon face and show what a profound impact these decisions have on your future. These examples highlight the importance of doing your research.

Many young adults fail to connect *how student loan payments affect their ability to invest young.* When are student loan payments made? During a young adult's most valuable investment years, or their twenties. High student loan payments can easily be the difference between investing and not investing for most of someone's twenties. As we saw with Kate in Chapter 2, high student loan debt that prevents someone from investing in their twenties can easily cut their lifetime worth by two-thirds and make becoming a millionaire nearly impossible. This chapter takes a few post-high school decisions and shows you how the numbers work out. Why is this important? So you can see the big picture and the outcomes of your post-high school decisions before signing on the dotted line.

Your research will help you preemptively avoid one of the biggest financial mistakes so many people make: selecting a career that is not stable or graduating with an expensive degree and living paycheck to paycheck in your twenties *to pay it off.* We want you to avoid all the common financial land mines out there because, quite frankly, young adults don't usually think about them and, unfortunately, regularly step on them. So, this chapter's main takeaway is this: If you don't want to be a dumba$$, **run the numbers for what you plan to do post-high school before making any decisions.** If any post-high school education is required, obtain it at the *lowest cost.* Why go to an expensive out-of-state or private school if cheaper options are available? As you'll soon see, saving a few hundred dollars a month on student loan payments will make a substantial difference in your long-term financial goals.

WHAT IS THE RELATIONSHIP BETWEEN EDUCATION LEVEL, SALARY, AND UNEMPLOYMENT RATE?

Generally speaking, going to college or completing higher education increases your lifetime earning power and decreases your unemployment rate. According to the US Bureau of Labor, the 2019 median annual salary and the unemployment rate for various education levels is as follows:

Education Level	Median Annual Salary	Median Monthly Salary	Unemployment Rate
Doctoral Degree	$97,916	$8,160	1.1%
Master's Degree	$77,844	$6,487	2.0%
Bachelor's Degree	$64,896	$5,408	2.2%
Associate Degree	$46,124	$3,844	2.7%
Some College, No Degree	$43,316	$3,610	3.3%
High School Diploma	$38,792	$3,233	3.7%
Less than High School Diploma	$30,784	$2,565	5.4%

Table 13. Median Annual Salary and Unemployment Rate for Different Education Levels[16]

The data suggest that the higher the education level, the higher the median salary and the lower the unemployment rate. It is also worth pointing out that the above data was from 2019, when the economy was

16.   "Learn More, Earn More: Education Leads to Higher Wages, Lower Unemployment." U.S. Bureau of Labor Statistics, May 2020. https://www.bls.gov/careeroutlook/2020/data-on-display/education-pays.htm.

strong, and salaries and unemployment numbers can fluctuate when the economy changes. However, as you'll soon see, not all majors are created equal. So, don't think that getting a master's degree in museum art management has the same annual salary and unemployment rate as a master's degree in computer engineering.

Next, let's take a closer look at various career options.

OPTION 1: IMMEDIATELY JOIN THE WORKFORCE

According to Admissionsly.com, in 2019, 33.8% of high school graduates did not immediately go to college.[17] So, it's important to discuss financial options that roughly one in three high school graduates face. Let's start by addressing a common misconception: You have to go to college or get an advanced degree to be a millionaire. When it comes to being a millionaire, *your education level may not have as much of an impact as you might think*. While someone who doesn't go to college may not make as much money over their lifetime as someone with higher education, they have two significant advantages that are often ignored: *more investment time* and *no student loan debt*.

Statistically speaking, yes, most likely someone with a high school diploma will not make as much money over their lifetime as someone with a college or advanced degree. However, there are tradeoffs with obtaining higher education. Those who choose to work immediately after

[**FAKE NEWS**]

You have to go to a four-year college to be a millionaire

---

17.   Vlsaova, Helen. "What Percent of High School Graduates Go to College? (Facts & Figures)" Admissonsly, November 21, 2020. https://admissionsly.com/percentage-who-go-to-college.

high school and do not go to college are not necessarily as financially worse off *in the long run* than someone who goes to college or has an advanced college degree. You may be saying to yourself, "That doesn't make any sense because how can someone making $38,792 a year not be as financially worse off in the long run as someone making $97,916 a year?"

What's a benefit of not going to college? The ability to invest sooner. Someone going to college or attaining an advanced degree is studying for four or more years. What are they NOT doing? *Investing.* And they are missing out on their most valuable investment years. This is not to say that someone shouldn't go to college. We both went to college. But, we don't want people to think that you *have* to go to college in order to be financially successful. And we are pointing out that joining the workforce immediately does offer an advantage.

Someone who chooses to enter the workforce *can invest immediately.* Remember, time turns a little bit of money into a lot of money. For example, high school diploma graduates enter the workforce at age eighteen or nineteen and invest four years earlier than most college graduates, six years earlier than most master's degrees, and nine years earlier than most doctoral degrees. So, while high school diplomas usually make less, *they make up for their lower income by investing earlier.* Meanwhile, college or advanced degree students make up for lost investment time with, on average, a higher median salary, lower unemployment, and a greater lifetime earning potential.

So, how do the numbers look? Does someone with a high school diploma or an associate degree mean that they can't be a millionaire because their salary is half of someone with an advanced degree? Table 14 shows various education levels, different starting investing ages based on when the education is done, and how much investing 10% of their pre-taxed median salary used from the US Bureau of Labor's 2019 stats from Table 13 is worth at sixty, assuming the monthly investment stays consistent.

Education Level	Investing Starting Age	Monthly Investment	Total Investment	Value at 60
High School Diploma	19	$323	$159,047	$1,176,342
Associate's	21	$384	$179,884	$1,190,260
Bachelor's	23	$541	$240,115	$1,423,273
Master's	25	$649	$272,454	$1,448,694
Doctoral	28	$816	$313,331	$1,419,299

Table 14. Investing 10% of Pre-Taxed Median Salary and Value at Sixty.

The table shows that *all education levels can be millionaires at sixty.* The difference between someone with a high school diploma and a doctoral who invests 10% of their median pre-tax salary is not as drastic as many may think. By having more time, in this case, nine more years, someone who joins the workforce immediately after high school and invests a total of $159,047 can reach above a million dollars. Meanwhile, doctoral degrees that invest $313,331 or roughly twice as much as a high school diploma earn only 21% more. What advantage did the high school diploma have over college or advanced degrees? *Time, precisely nine more years.* Yes, someone with a master's or doctoral degree will most likely make more money over a lifetime and possibly invest more money than what is shown in the table. However, this book is about making everyone a millionaire, and as the table confirms, *everyone, regardless of education level, can be a millionaire* if the correct actions are taken.

The second advantage for those who enter the workforce is they don't have student debt. Table 14's data on education level versus salary does not list the average student loan debt and how much each degree earns *after paying off mandatory student loans.* Most likely, someone with a higher degree and salary has student loan debt, which subtracts from their investment ability. Some may be *investing less than someone with a high school diploma* due to their high student loan payment and end up with less in the long term. In the end, the annual salary and education level table are misleading because it omits student loan debt.

While someone going straight into the workforce can invest immediately and does not have student loan debt, one important drawback is someone without higher education has a higher unemployment rate. This means there may be periods of unemployment and no investment. Thus, there is no way to factor in job stability in calculations, but we wanted to ensure you were aware of it. Thus, consistent investment money throughout one's late teens and twenties may be challenging for some with a high school diploma.

Still, the bottom line is you don't have to go to college to be a millionaire as long as you consistently invest at least 10% of your salary *starting immediately.* Those who choose not to attend college or post-secondary training have two significant advantages. The first is no student loan debt, which subtracts from your paycheck and investment money. The second is more time to turn a little money into a lot.

OPTION 2: ATTEND A FOUR-YEAR COLLEGE

According to Admissionsly.com, 66.2% of high school graduates immediately enrolled in college in 2019.[18] So, roughly two out of three high school graduates make the biggest financial decision before they are even legal adults. The cost of higher education is the most overlooked aspect of young adult financial planning and is a primary reason why some young adults get financially derailed. Sadly, some never recover from it. Many assume that everything will "work out" after college, and they will make enough money to pay for a certain lifestyle and their

18.   Ibid.

DID YOU KNOW?

Student loan debt is the only debt that is not automatically forgiven in bankruptcy court—meaning it is very hard to get rid of.

student loan payment, only to find out later that their financial situation is not as strong as they'd hoped. However, by that time, for many, it is too late. The financial damage has already been done. What's alarming is that roughly 14.5 million college graduates couldn't find a job in a field that their major is in.[19] Remember, *your student loan payments are due whether you get a job or not, and they stay with you until they are paid off.* And, your student loans can be one of your highest monthly expenses if not considered carefully.

As we mentioned earlier, there are countless possibilities for what a four-year degree could cost you. For example, you may have a partial or full-ride scholarship, or maybe your parents help pay for some or all of your tuition costs, you work part-time to help pay tuition, you may go out-of-state, in-state, private, or receive a tuition discount, use a grant or one of the nearly infinite combinations… regardless, we can't predict what your cost will be. Still, we can show you the importance of understanding the future financial implications of your decisions. In addition, college costs continue to fluctuate. Below, we use May 2021 tuition rates provided on the colleges' website for all examples.

---

19.   McDermott, Jennifer. "Why 2 in 5 Americans Don't See Value in Their College Degree." finder, February 9, 2021. https://www.finder.com/college-degree-value.

First, let's examine how something as simple as going in-state or out-of-state affects your ability to become a millionaire. Meet Hadley and Jackson, who

attend the same high school in Virginia. Both want to go to a four-year university and major in biology. Jackson attends the University of South Carolina and pays $33,928 a year for out-of-state tuition or $135,712 for his four-year biology degree.[20] Meanwhile, Hadley attends Virginia Tech and pays $13,691 a year for in-state tuition or $54,992 for her four-year biology degree.[21] Jackson pays $20,237 more each year or $80,948 to attend South Carolina *for the same degree* as Hadley.

After graduation, Hadley and Jackson get hired by the same biotechnology firm with roughly the *same starting salary*. However, shortly after getting hired, they both receive their first student loan payment bill. How different are they?

Student	Total Loan Amount	Monthly Student Loan Payment	Interest Paid	Accumulative Payment
Hadley (In-State)	$54,992	$605	$17,610	$72,602
Jackson (Out-of-State)	$135,712	$1,493	$43,458	$179,170
Difference	**$80,720**	**$888**	**$25,848**	**$106,568**

Table 15. In-State and Out-of-State Payments with a Ten-Year, 5.8% Interest Rate

According to Table 15, Jackson has an *$888 higher student loan payment over ten years* than Hadley because he attended an out-of-state

20.   "Tuition and Aid." University of South Carolina, accessed May 14, 2021. https://www.sc.edu/apply/tuition-aid/index.php.
21.   "Expenses & Financial Aid." Virginia Tech, accessed January 12, 2022. https://vt.edu/admissions/undergraduate/cost.html.

school. Even though he's earning roughly the same salary after college, Jackson will have a much steeper hill to climb to become a millionaire since he has substantially higher student loans. Not only are his student loans higher, but he's also severely damaging his financial future because his higher student loan payments make it difficult for him to invest in *his most valuable investment years.* Whether a frog's anatomy is taught at Virginia Tech or South Carolina, the course material is mostly the same. Both get a bachelor's degree in science. Both get a piece of paper saying they met the university's degree requirements. *So why would someone pay two to three times more to learn the same information and earn roughly the same salary?* Ask yourself this, "Would you rather be a biologist earning $60,000 while paying off $135,712 of student loan debt or $54,992 of student loan debt?"

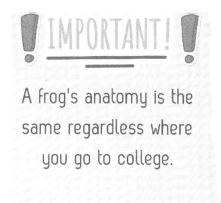

IMPORTANT!

A frog's anatomy is the same regardless where you go to college.

What are the long-term financial impacts of Jackson's decision versus Hadley's? Pretend Hadley invests her $888 a month savings from attending an in-state college that Jackson isn't able to afford because he went out of state. How much more money would Hadley have at age sixty and seventy? Age sixty: **$1,438,297**. Age seventy: **$3,105,175**.

Something as trivial as going in-state versus out-of-state college provides Hadley the opportunity to earn an additional $1.4 million by age sixty and $3.1 million by age seventy more than Jackson. *That decision alone is a million-dollar decision.* Meanwhile, Jackson will most likely have to wait years until he earns enough to pay his $1,493 monthly college loan payment *and invest.* What's worse is Jackson is not capitalizing on his most valuable investment years because he wanted to go out of state when a more practical alternative was available. Unless your degree isn't offered at an in-state university or because of scholarships, why would anyone even consider attending an out-of-state university?

What did we learn from Hadley and Jackson? Their scenario highlights that something as common as where you go to college greatly impacts your ability to be a millionaire. Hadley comes out of college at a significant financial advantage compared to Jackson. Both graduated with the same degree, but their student loan payments set them on two different financial paths. Some employers pay the same starting salary regardless of where you went to school. For example, most government jobs, including military officers and teachers, are paid the same regardless of where the hiree attended school. So why would you spend two to three times for a degree that pays the same amount? What does the higher price tag get *you*?

Another four-year option is to attend a private college. Private four-year colleges also provide an opportunity to get a four-year degree. Private schools are attractive because most offer smaller class sizes compared to larger public universities. According to a 2019 US World News survey, the national average tuition for one year at a private college was $35,676, compared to $9,716 for in-state and $21,629 for out-of-

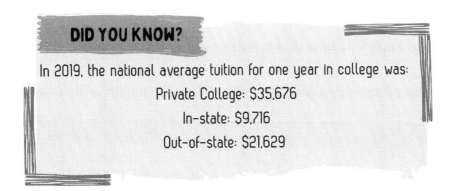

DID YOU KNOW?

In 2019, the national average tuition for one year in college was:
Private College: $35,676
In-state: $9,716
Out-of-state: $21,629

state.[22] It is important to note that many private colleges offer tuition discounts to students, sometimes as high as 50%. However, the private university tuition widely ranges, and for the examples in this book, we use the $35,676 national average above. Clearly, there are price-tag differences nationally, but depending upon your situation (receiving a private university discount or parents providing assistance), your numbers will be different, which is why it's important to understand the financial consequences of your education decisions before committing.

How much will your monthly payment be after college using these average national tuition rates without considering any parental assistance, scholarships, or discounts?

Education	Four-Year Tuition Cost	Monthly Student Loan Payment	Total Payment
Public in-state	$38,864	$428	$51,309
Public out-of-state	$86,516	$941	$112,900
Private	$142,704	$1,570	$188,401

Table 16. Four-Year College Costs with a Ten-Year, 5.8% Interest Rate

Obtaining a four-year degree is a significant investment, and clearly, some options are more expensive than others. As seen in Table 16, attending a private university over an in-state university could result in roughly a $1,100 higher monthly student loan payment over ten years, resulting in significantly less investment money in your twenties. High student loan payments are a major reason why some students who attend expensive colleges have difficulty investing any money in their twenties—because most of their income is spent paying off college debt rather than investing. They could have cut their college debt in half or more by attending a more affordable option. Spending more money for

22.   Kerr, Emma, and Sarah Wood. "The Cost of Private vs. Public Colleges." June 8, 2022. https://www.usnews.com/education/best-colleges/paying-for-college/articles/2019-06-25/the-cost-of-private-vs-public-colleges.

the same degree just doesn't make financial sense in most situations. When was the last time you looked at job postings and saw one that read, "private or out-of-state four-year degree" required? Most likely never. All that matters is that a degree is completed. What you pay for it is *your choice*.

The final path we discuss to a four-year degree is to attend the first two years at a community college and then transfer to a four-year university. How much money do two years at a community college save you? Let's compare Hadley and Jackson again, who now want to major in finance. Hadley attends community college for the first two years and transfers to James Madison University (JMU) for the final two years and graduates. According to Education Data, in 2019, the national average for in-state community college tuition costs $4,220 a year, and JMU's in-state tuition costs $12,250 a year.[23, 24] Hadley's first two years at a community college cost her $8,440, and her final two years at JMU cost her $24,500. Hadley's finance degree costs her $32,940 total. Meanwhile, Jackson attends JMU for four years and graduates with a finance degree and $49,000 in student loan debt. Hadley and Jackson both have a JMU degree and *equal employment prospects*; however, by going to community college first, Hadley saved $16,060, decreasing her monthly college debt payment by $177.

23.   Hanson, Melanie. "Average Cost of Community College." Education Data Initiative, January 27, 2021. https://educationdata.org/average-cost-of-community-college.

24.   "Tuition, Financial Aid & Scholarships." James Madison University, accessed May 16, 2022. https://www.jmu.edu/admissions/tuition-financial-aid-and-scholarships.shtml.

	Total Loan Amount	Monthly Student Loan Payment	Accumulative Payment
Hadley (Community College + JMU)	$32,940	$362	$43,488
Jackson (JMU only)	$49,000	$539	$64,691
Difference	**$16,060**	**$177**	**$21,203**

Table 17. Community College and Four-Year Universities Comparison with a Ten-Year, 5.8% Interest Rate

As a quick side note, some of you might be lucky enough to have your parents pay for your college education, or maybe you will get a full-ride scholarship. In either of these situations, you could graduate debt-free. What should you do then? Just as we have been saying all along, start investing as young as possible and budget your money in order to invest.

"THE COLLEGE EXPERIENCE"—IS IT REALLY THAT MAGICAL?

Some of you may think that there is no way you will do anything but go to a four-year college because you want the full "college" experience, and you don't care how much it costs. However, according to Forbes, "A mere 2 out of 100 students ultimately experienced the true magic of college."[25] We are not sure what "magic" you are hoping for… parties, dorm life, sports events, sororities/fraternities, college clubs… Maybe you feel peer pressure to get the full college experience. Either way, the idea that you go to college hoping for something that "2 out of 100" experience and that is clearly not for the majority of people might be something to think about. Again, if you are lucky enough to have

---

25.   Busteed, Brandon. "The True 'Magic' of College Happens for Just 2 out of 100 Students." Forbes, August 22, 2020. https://www.forbes.com/sites/brandonbusteed/2020/08/22/the-true-magic-of-college-happens-for-just-2-out-of-100-students/?sh=cd138f21d2f7.

college paid for by family or scholarships, this is not a consideration. But for those of you who do have to pay for college, think about what you want for what you are paying. The degree is what is going to make you money, not the memories of your first keg stand. Also, we are willing to bet that there are plenty of four-year colleges that are affordable and still offer you the "magic" of college. Bottom line: Don't spend a bunch of money hoping to experience something that 98 out of 100 do not.

LET'S PAUSE AND RECAP SO FAR...

There are many routes to a four-year degree. You can go to a traditional state school in-state or out-of-state. You can attend a private school. Or, you can do a combo of community college and then a four-year university. As we showed, the costs differ depending on the route you take. We did not talk about those who obtained scholarships or graduated debt-free because they worked while in school or their parents helped them. According to ThinkImpact.com, in 2020, there were over 1.7 million scholarships available in the US.[26] We do not address this because there are countless variations. Our best advice is that if you are lucky enough to graduate debt-free or with less debt than the above examples, then it will greatly help your chances of investing young and improve your chances of becoming a millionaire. Remember, the sooner you begin investing, the easier it is to become one. One of the biggest hindrances is student loan debt, and doing everything possible to have as little student loan debt as possible should be a top priority.

---

26. "Scholarship Statistics." ThinkImpact, accessed November 10, 2021. https://www.thinkimpact.com/scholarship-statistics/#:~:text=Report%20Highlights%3A,aid%20to%207.5%20million%20students.

OPTION 3: TRADE SCHOOL, ASSOCIATE DEGREE (COMMUNITY COLLEGE), OR CERTIFICATIONS/APPRENTICESHIPS

Trade schools, community colleges, and apprenticeships do not get the credit and respect they deserve. Society perpetuates a narrative that everyone must go to college to succeed in life, but this couldn't be further from the truth because college is not for everyone and often isn't needed. Did you know that 27% of students who attend trade school earn more than the average person with a bachelor's degree?[27] Any vocational route *costs a fraction of what four-year universities cost, they are shorter to complete, some pay more than bachelor's degrees, and many have lower unemployment rates.*

DID YOU KNOW?

27% of students who attend trade school earn more than the average person with a bachelor's degree.

What is a trade school?

A trade school is a training program where you learn a vocational career such as carpentry, appliance repair, automotive maintenance, plumbing, cosmetology, culinary arts, and many more options. Some programs can be completed in weeks or months, while others may take

---

27.   Gaille, Louise. "Trade School vs. College: The Big Pros and Cons for Each." Vittana.org, June 24, 2019. https://vittana.org/trade-school-vs-college-the-big-pros-and-cons-for-each.

two years. Tuition fees range from around $5,000 to $10,000 per year and vary depending on the type of institution you attend, the program you choose, and whether you attend a public or private program.[28] After graduating from a trade school, you receive a vocational certificate in a specialized field to enter the workforce.

What is an associate degree?

An associate degree is a two-year program offered at a community college in which you are trained for a specific vocational skill. These programs skip the expensive humanities, liberal arts, and ethnic studies requirements that most four-year universities require. Doing so allows the student to go right into the classes in their specialized field. Many programs are available, including occupational therapy, surgical technology, and radiation therapy. What is the goal? To graduate in two years and be prepared for immediate employment. The national average cost in 2020 for an associate's degree was $3,570 per year.[29]

What is an apprenticeship?

An apprenticeship is an opportunity in which a company hires you to work and, in turn, trains you for a specific job. They are a unique training opportunity that is *usually free and allows people to learn new skills while getting paid.* Apprenticeships and other trainee opportunities are a great path to new full-time careers and developmental

NOTE TO SELF

"Some vocational jobs pay around the same as four-year degrees but cost a fraction of the price and take less time to complete."

28.   Miller, Scott. "The Average Cost of Vocational School in USA 2022." Vocational Training HQ, February 16, 2022. https://www.vocationaltraininghq.com/average-cost-vocational-school-usa-2017/.

29.   "The Average Cost of College in 2020." USA Student Debt Relief, October 6, 2020. https://usastudentdebtrelief.com/the-average-cost-of-college-in-2020/.

opportunities. In FY2021, there were over 593,000 apprentices in the US with companies like Walmart, CVS, Boyd Gaming, Groove Entertainment Technologies, and IBM.[30] Countless companies offer opportunities to get paid while learning a marketable skill. If this sounds like something you are interested in, you should start looking at options on apprenticeship.gov. With a quick search, you'll find apprenticeship information, available opportunities, and expected salaries in your area.

Option 3 is attractive because *some vocational jobs pay around the same as four-year degrees but cost a fraction of the price and take less time to complete.* A community college or trade school graduate comes out of their program with a comparable salary yet less debt. They have more flexibility to invest in their twenties.

Starting two years earlier will have significant future benefits. How much of a difference? Let's run the numbers with our friends Hadley and Jackson again. This time, Jackson graduates from community college at age twenty-one and invests $300 a month from age twenty-one to age sixty. Hadley graduates from a four-year university at age twenty-three and invests $300 a month from age twenty-three to age sixty. How much will Jackson and Hadley each have at age sixty?

	Investing Starting Age	Total Invested	Value at 60	Difference
Jackson (Community College)	21	$140,400	$929,004	$139,467
Hadley (Four-Year University)	23	$133,200	$789,537	

Table 18. Investing $300 a Month After Community College Versus Obtaining a Bachelor's Degree

---

30.   "FY 2021 Data and Statistics." United States Department of Labor, accessed May 16, 2021. https://www.dol.gov/agencies/eta/apprenticeship/about/statistics/2021.

Jackson will have $139,467 more than Hadley by completing vocational training, getting a job, and investing *two years earlier.* Remember, *the earlier you invest, the more it will be worth.*

In addition, many community college programs and trade schools keep pace with the economy and offer programs that are directly applicable to the workforce. Meanwhile, the same cannot be said for all four-year degrees. From a marketable career perspective, *some liberal arts and humanities degrees had limited value thirty years ago, have limited value today, and will continue to have limited value in the future,* yet many college students continue majoring in them. While this may be disheartening to some of our readers, motivating everyone to believe that they will be the next Smithsonian Museum Director or Mandy Moore is misleading and actually setting some people up for a life of disappointment. Again, it is your life, and you will decide to do what you want, BUT, at least by reading this, you have more information regarding finances and how money works compared to before. In the end, the choice is ultimately yours with what you choose to do with this information.

IMPORTANT!

Not every house needs an anthropology or psychology major, but every house needs a plumber and electrician.

If getting a vocational certificate or associate degree interests you, research the various vocational jobs available, the cost and duration of the training, the salary, and employment opportunities. The best place to start is the Bureau of Labor and Statistics website, bls.gov.

So, which is better? A trade school? An associate degree? An apprenticeship? The better option is the one that fits your life goals. So, we leave you with this thought: *Not every house needs an anthropology or psychology major, but every house needs an electrician and plumber.* In other words, some trade school degrees are usually more marketable than some four-year majors.

OPTION 4: JOIN THE MILITARY

Joining the military provides many benefits and is another option to either help pay for college or receive paid training. We will only provide a quick overview of information and not go into too much detail on military benefits; however, if joining the military interests you, please do additional research or consider contacting an armed service recruiter for more information. We will focus on the financial benefits of why you should consider joining the military.

Enlist at eighteen–
Retire at thirty-eight.
Commission at twenty-two–
Retire at forty-two.

POINT TO PONDER

Benefit 1: Paid College Tuition. A primary reason why many young adults join the military, including one of this book's authors, is for the education benefits. There are several ways to get college tuition covered, including serving part-time by joining either the National Guard or the Reserves. You can also get college tuition paid for by joining your college's Reserve Officer Training Corps (ROTC) program. After graduation, your service commitment is fulfilled as an officer on active duty for four years for most careers. Finally, you can also attend one of the Service Academies such as West Point or the Air Force Academy free of charge. Like ROTC, your service commitment is fulfilled by serving as an officer on active duty after graduation.

Benefit 2: Free Training. The military trains and pays its service members to learn a specific profession. The military offers hundreds of career options, including being a pilot, law enforcement, dental hygienist, doctor, x-ray technician, mechanic, engineer, and many others paid for by the military at no cost to the service member. Then, when their service commitment is over, they can take all training qualifications/certifications to the civilian world.

Benefit 3: Job Security. In the civilian world, jobs and companies are sensitive to downsizing, restructuring, changes, and the economy's strength. However, national defense has been around for thousands of years and will likely continue to be a top priority for many years

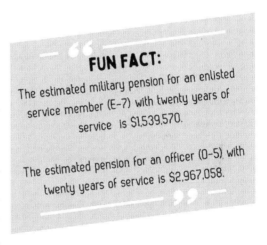

FUN FACT:
The estimated military pension for an enlisted service member (E-7) with twenty years of service is $1,539,570.

The estimated pension for an officer (O-5) with twenty years of service is $2,967,058.

to come. Thus, service members have high job security and a nearly-guaranteed paycheck until the service commitment expires.

Benefit 4: Pension. The military has an outstanding pension for service members who serve at least twenty years. Active-duty members *receive 40% of their base salary immediately after retiring and receive a monthly pension for the rest of their lives after twenty years of service.* Enlisted members can begin collecting this pension as early as thirty-eight years old, while officers can begin collecting their pension as early as forty-two. The pension goes up by 2% a year for each additional year served beyond twenty years, so serving twenty-five years would result in a pension of 50% of the service member's base pay. Meanwhile, guard or reserve members receive their pension at age sixty, and the value is based on a point system determined by the number of drills and days served. In addition, military retirees also receive affordable healthcare for themselves, their spouse, and any minor dependents for the rest of their lives. Additional active-duty financial benefits include:

- Base pay based on grade and years of service, tax-free monthly housing, and food allowance
- Free healthcare and dental—family members receive a low, subsidized rate.
- Veterans Affair Loan Eligibility (buy a house with 0% down)
- Matching 401K (Thrift Savings Plan) up to 5% and a mid-career bonus
- The Post-9/11 GI Bill (four-year college tuition paid and is transferrable to immediate family)
- Thirty days of vacation a year, and Federal Holidays and Family Days (additional twenty-two days off)

HOW MUCH IS HAVING THE MILITARY PAY FOR YOUR SCHOOL WORTH?

Let's now pretend Jackson is a Wisconsin resident and wants to attend the University of Wisconsin (UW). For the academic year 2022-23, UW had a $10,796.40 annual tuition rate and fees for residents.[31] For simplicity, we'll assume the tuition rate stays the same for all four years, so the total for a four-year degree is $43,185.60. If Jackson had to

---

31.   "Tuition Rates." Bursar's Office, accessed May 4, 2021. https://bursar.wisc.edu/tuition-and-fees/tuition-rates.

pay for all four years of college without any scholarships, his monthly student loan payment would be $475 for ten years. But instead, Jackson decides to join the National Guard to pay for his education. After four years, he graduates from UW with no student loan debt, and instead of paying a $475 monthly student loan, he invests it.

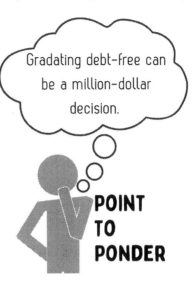

Gradating debt-free can be a million-dollar decision.

POINT TO PONDER

By joining the National Guard and graduating debt-free, how much will Jackson be worth at sixty and seventy by investing his would-be student loan payment rather than paying it?

Age sixty: $712,370   **Age seventy: $1,537,952**

If he had invested his tuition savings, Jackson's decision to join the military would have been worth $712,370 more at age sixty and a little more than $1.5 million at age seventy by having the military pay for his college and investing the savings. So, if you join the military, you are not only joining the world's most elite military and learning essential life skills, but you are also adding roughly $1.5 million to your future net worth at age seventy, assuming you invest the college loan savings. *Having the military pay for your college and graduating debt-free is literally a million-dollar decision.*

Of course, some students are more privileged than others, and they may graduate debt-free for any other reason, such as non-military scholarships or because their parents helped them financially. If this should happen in your case, your financial future would be similar to the example above, assuming you invest the same amount for the first ten years after college. Always remember, being *debt-free* and *investing early* are huge steps in becoming a millionaire.

HOW YOUR CAREER AFFECTS BECOMING A MILLIONAIRE

Clearly, after running the numbers, the main objective of choosing a career is balancing something that interests you, but more importantly, salary and employment prospects. For example, managing art museums may be of interest to you, but the chances of getting hired are extremely small. So, if you pursue higher education, a good return on your education investment is needed. But, in the end, the decision is ultimately yours. Of course, some of you will still choose to chase the dream job. But, for some majors, you have to be okay that you may not make as much as you need for the lifestyle you want. Or, you may work a few jobs to get to the dream job.

According to a 2019 survey by Labor Market and Research of College Graduates, 28.2% of college graduates said they could not find a job in the field they got a degree.[32] As this stat shows, *nearly one in four college graduates cannot find a job* after investing tens of thousands of dollars. In addition, *53.2 million Americans say their college degree wasn't worth the money they spent attaining it.*[33] Of course, not everyone's goal in life is to be a millionaire, but if theirs is

SAD FACT:
28.2% of college graduates said they could not find a job in the field they got a degree.

---

32.   McDermott, Jennifer. "Why 2 in 5 Americans Don't See Value in Their College Degree." finder, February 9, 2021. https://www.finder.com/college-degree-value.
33.   Ibid.

and they choose a career with low prospects, what are their chances of becoming one? Not high. They might as well have skipped college, saved tens of thousands of dollars, and gone straight to flipping burgers. Thus, it is critical to not only choose a cost-effective form of education but a career that provides you with a high chance of success after graduation because the career you choose matters and should not be taken lightly. What careers should you consider? Which ones should you avoid? You should start by finding a job you're interested in, calculate the salary, and investment or education required.

Choosing an unmarketable major may result in returning for more education or training and having even higher student loans. You may need to accept a job you do not want just to earn a paycheck. You could be unemployed. We all have different interests and abilities, but society financially rewards those with marketable majors. That is the reality you must face.

We are not telling you what to do after high school; we are just suggesting that you understand your future financial situation before committing. *Do your research* in order to balance interests, salary, and employment prospects. Start planning it out now before reality hits you later. No one should be shocked when they graduate and either can't find a job in their chosen

NOTE TO SELF
❝Understand your future financial situation before committing.❞

career field or make a low salary. All the information is out there—you just have to use it to make a smart choice. Your career eventually determines what kind of house you can buy, the type of car you can drive, and the number of vacations you can afford.

HOW YOUR CAREER CAN GREATLY IMPACT YOUR FINANCIAL FUTURE

Let's do the math and compare two careers. We Googled top-earning and worst-earning careers and pulled one from each list. For this example, we'll compare the earning potential of a cybersecurity and rehabilitation counseling degree. In 2020, a rehabilitation counseling degree had an average starting salary of $38,000, while a cybersecurity degree had an average starting salary of $75,000.[34, 35] Meanwhile, the average mid-career salary for a rehabilitation counseling degree is $46,100, while the average mid-career salary for a cybersecurity degree is $116,000.[36, 37] Using the average mid-career salary and assuming someone enters the workforce at age twenty-three and retires at age sixty, how do the total lifetime earnings compare between these two degrees?

Major	Average Annual Salary	Years Worked	Total Lifetime Earnings
Rehabilitation Counseling	$46,100	37	$1,705,700
Cybersecurity	$116,000	37	$4,292,000
Difference			**+$2,586,300**

Table 19. Career-Earning Differences Between Cybersecurity and Rehabilitation Counseling

---

34.   Cromwelle, Joy. "30 Best College Majors for the Future [2022 Rankings]." MyDegreeGuide, December 2, 2021. https://www.mydegreeguide.com/best-college-majors/.

35.   Fischer, Michael S. "20 Worst Paying College Majors (That Aren't Education): 2020." ThinkAdvisor, October 12, 2020. https://www.thinkadvisor.com/2020/10/12/20-worst-paying-college-majors-that-arent-education-2020/.

36.   Cromwelle, Joy. "30 Best College Majors for the Future [2022 Rankings]." MyDegreeGuide.com, December 2, 2021. https://www.mydegreeguide.com/best-college-majors/.

37.   Fischer, Michael S. "20 Worst Paying College Majors (That Aren't Education): 2020." ThinkAdvisor, October 12, 2020. https://www.thinkadvisor.com/2020/10/12/20-worst-paying-college-majors-that-arent-education-2020/.

Majoring in cybersecurity will likely earn someone slightly more than $2.5 million over their lifetime than rehabilitation counseling. This means the cybersecurity major can take more vacations, live in a bigger house, and invest more. As this example demonstrates, there is a drastic difference between lifetime earnings based on your chosen career. Both majors went to a four-year university and paid the same tuition amount; however, *one earns $2.5 million more over a lifetime*. The question is, why would you not want to choose a career that provides a high return on investment and possibly maximizes your potential lifetime earnings? While we all have different interests and skill levels, a profession's annual pay and prospects should be strongly considered. Remember, a *four-year college costs the same regardless of your major*. The question is, do you want to earn $40,000, $50,000, $60,000, or $70,000 as a starting salary after graduation?

PUTTING IT ALL TOGETHER—EDUCATION, SALARY, AND BECOMING A MILLIONAIRE

So far, this chapter has looked at different degrees, education options, and how different career choices affect your ability to invest while young. It's time to put it all together and make sense of it. It's time to show how your student loan payments, based on where you go or will go to school, and your chosen career and salary, impact your ability to be a millionaire.

At this point, you most likely have some sense of what career you want to pursue and, if any higher education is required, where you'd like to go to school. Hopefully, you know what kind of salary your career pays, how much any higher education would cost, and your monthly payments. To tie together salary, student loan debt, and how it impacts your ability to invest young, which is key to becoming a millionaire, we constructed Table 20 using three starting salaries: $40,000, $55,000, and $70,000. We also included different scenarios for the roughly 33% of high school graduates who go directly into the workforce after graduation and also examined someone who makes $10, $15, and $20 an hour working full time after high school.

For each scenario, we calculated how much money was left over after taxes were withheld and monthly student loan payments were paid. When calculating this example's monthly student loan payment, we used a 25% tax rate to cover federal, state, and social security taxes and a ten-year, 5.8% interest loan payment. For all examples, we used the national average tuition rates for all four-year universities and community colleges and did not include financial aid or scholarships. The amount of money left over after paying taxes and student loan payments, also referred to as the monthly leftover income, was then arranged from highest to lowest. Let's look and see how salary and student loan payments impact financials for a recent college graduate.

Annual Salary	Monthly Income (after 25% Tax Rate)	Highest Completed Education Level	Monthly Student Loan Payment	Monthly Income after Paying Student Loan and Taxes
$70,000	$4,375	Community College	$84	**$4,291**
$70,000	$4,375	In-State, Four-Year	$428	**$3,947**
$70,000	$4,375	Out-of-State, Four-Year	$941	**$3,434**
$55,000	$3,438	Community College	$84	**$3,354**
$55,000	$3,438	In-State, Four-Year	$428	**$3,010**

$70,000	$4,375	Private, Four-Year	$1,570	**$2,805**
$20/Hour	$2,520	High School Diploma	$0	**$2,520**
$55,000	$3,438	Out-of-State, Four-Year	$941	**$2,497**
$40,000	$2,500	Community College	$84	**$2,416**
$40,000	$2,500	In-State, Four-Year	$428	**$2,072**
$15/Hour	$1,890	High School Diploma	$0	**$1,890**
$55,000	$3,438	Private, Four-Year	$1,570	**$1,868**
$40,000	$2,500	Out-of-State, Four-Year	$941	**$1,559**
$10/Hour	$1,260	High School Diploma	$0	**$1,260**
$40,000	$2,500	Private, Four-Year	$1,570	**$930**

Table 20. Salary and Student Loan Payments Impact on Your Monthly Income

Take some time to look at the various financial scenarios above. Pay particular attention to how expensive forms of higher education (out-of-state and private university) reduces your monthly income compared to more affordable forms of higher education (in-state or community college). Generally speaking, expensive higher forms of education are in the middle to lower half of the table, meaning they make *less money* after paying their loans. In contrast, more affordable forms of education tend to be in the upper to the middle half of the table, meaning they make *more money* after paying their loans. The chart gives a potential sneak peek of what your financial future *could be* like based on your career and where you go to school. Here are some interesting points to consider:

- Someone who attends a private university and then gets a job with a $70,000 salary makes about $300 more a month than a high school graduate working full time and earning $20 an hour.

- Someone who attends a private university and then gets a job with a $55,000 salary has $1,868 to live off each month after paying student loan payments.

- Someone who skips college and gets a job earning $20/hour makes *more money* than someone who attends an out-of-state or private university and gets a job with a $55,000 salary.

While the table above assumes no financial aid or scholarships, many college students receive some sort of financial assistance. In those cases, the monthly student loan payment would be lower, and the monthly leftover income would be higher. Scholarship or no scholarship, it's important to understand the relationship between student loan payments and your ability to invest young.

Now, think about the scenarios we have discussed. Could you afford to pay the bills and invest? When planning your future, don't just be familiar with how much your job should make, but *how much your job should make after paying student loan payments or your living expenses.* With the goal of being a millionaire, you want to pick a path with the highest probability of achieving it. Clearly, it's not attending a private university for a major that pays $40,000 a year. How can you possibly pay your bills and still invest if your take home pay is $930 a month after paying off your student loan payment? That may not even be enough to cover your rent!

As we said from the beginning, the easiest way to be a millionaire is to invest young, and this table shows how difficult investing young can be depending on your major and where you go to school. *Tomorrow's finances are based on decisions made today*. While education and career routes can seem like a black box of unknowns, one certain thing is the math doesn't lie—the numbers provide a preview into your future.

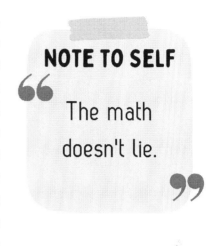

The good news is there are many great-paying jobs. Some require college, while others may not. But what if you want to follow your dreams of being an interpretative dance major? That's great! But will an interpretative dance major make enough money after college to repay the loans and invest? Probably not. You may have to choose between making dance a hobby versus a career. Which is more important to you? By researching and running the numbers, you should find a solution that fits your needs and wants for your future.

MY COLLEGE WAS PAID FOR—HOW DO I BENEFIT?

Some of you reading this book may have had or will have college paid for, either from parents, relatives, or maybe even a scholarship. Now what? First off, it's essential to recognize the tremendous gift and opportunity you have been given. If your parents, a family member, or an organization paid for your school, take a minute to write them a handwritten thank you note. Because of them, you are in the most ideal position to become not just a millionaire but a *multi-millionaire…*

IF you choose to continue your good fortunes and aggressively invest after graduation.

Instead of paying hundreds or even thousands towards *student loans* every month, you have an *opportunity* to instead put hundreds or even thousands on *investments* every month... *in your early twenties.* But again, what you do is ultimately *your decision.* Do you want to squash this tremendous opportunity and not invest, or do you want to make the most of your good fortunes and become a multi-millionaire?

How much money could you have at age sixty if you increase your investment? From Chapter 2, Kate had $789,537 by investing $300 a month from age twenty-three to sixty. What if Kate graduated college without any student loan debt because she either received a full-ride scholarship or her parents paid for school? Instead of investing $300 a month, Kate can now afford to invest $800 or even $1,000 a month because she has no student loan payment. How much would she have at age sixty?

Scenario	Value at 60
Investing $300/Month from 23-60 (College Debt)	$789,537
Investing $800/Month from 23-60 (No College Debt)	$2,273,868
Investing $1,000/Month from 23-60 (No College Debt)	$2,842,335

Table 21. Kate's Investment of $800 and $1,000 a Month when Graduating Debt Free

As the table shows, by graduating debt-free, Kate can invest more each month because she doesn't have to make a college loan payment. Kate will be a *multi-millionaire* by investing $800 or $1,000 a month after college. This is again another reminder of the importance of *keeping your college loan debt to a minimum, even having no debt if possible, because of how powerful it is later in life.*

ARE YOU STILL WITH US?

As we stated at the beginning of this chapter, the main point was not to *tell you what to decide but to convince you to run the numbers beforehand.* First, decide what you want to do and how you will achieve it. Then, research the financial consequences of that decision. Maybe you want to be a dental hygienist? A doctor? A teacher? Go into the family business? A truck driver? The first thing you need to think of is how you will get there. If higher education is required, how much will it cost you? What are the employment prospects of that decision?

There are several routes to take. Some are more costly than others. *Before signing on any dotted line, understand the big financial picture.* Understand what your finances will look like after graduation. Estimate how much your monthly student loan payment will be, how long it will take to pay for it, how much your investment will be worth later in life, and whether or not your salary and debt incurred will allow you to invest. All of these numbers can easily be calculated.

The US Bureau of Labor Statistics is a great place to get started. There are articles and stats on nearly every career. By a simple search, you can learn the median salary, the unemployment rate, the type of degree you need, and so much more. It is the perfect place to get a snapshot of any career you consider. Yes, there are thousands of combinations:

OPERATION DON'T BE A DUMBA$$

Your Mission:
Choose a marketable career and obtain it with the lowest debt possible.

public, private, four-year, vocational training, community colleges, in-state, out-of-state, scholarships, grants, tuition discounts… it is overwhelming. But it doesn't have to be. Focus on the big picture: *To have money and invest young, you need to have a good-paying job, and if higher education is required, get it for as low a cost as possible.*

Yes, this stuff can be overwhelming and daunting, but this is where you decide how you choose to live your life and what kind of life you will have and what kind of life you want. Focus on what knowledge or skill you can acquire that is useful and needed in society. Focus on what expectations you have for your life. Focus on paying yourself. Focus on becoming a millionaire and not a dumba$$. And how do you do that? *Choose a marketable career and obtain it with the lowest debt possible.*

KEY TAKEAWAYS OF DECISION 4:

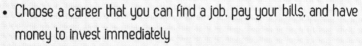

- Choose a career that you can find a job, pay your bills, and have money to invest immediately
- Get your training or degree for as little debt (if any) as possible
- Do your research and run the numbers

"You can have a masters degree in making money, but you will still wind up broke if you have a PhD in spending it."
-Orrin Woodward

"I played a lot of basketball growing up. Throughout high school and college, I had both Nike and non-brand-named athletic clothing that I wore when I played. But something dawned on me one day: When playing basketball, **I realized that I played the same whether I wore a $25 set of non-brand shirt and shorts or a $100 pair of Nike shirt and shorts**. My shooting, acceleration, dribbling, defense, and rebounding were the same regardless of what I wore. It should be obvious, but **how well someone plays is more about individual skill level than the price tag of one's clothing**. I will be the first to admit that my Nike clothes 'looked better' on me while playing. However, wearing the better-looking, four-times-more expensive Nike clothes did not allow me to dunk from the free-throw line like Jordan or always hit the game-winning shot like Kobe (RIP), as I had seen in their commercials. So, why do we pay so much more for a piece of athletic attire that, at best, provides minimal athletic performance improvement? We pay more because advertising and marketing have effectively programmed us to believe that **better versions of ourselves are obtainable only if we buy their product.** Buy the cologne to get the hot girl. Buy this expensive handbag, and you'll be happy and have a lot of friends. Buy this sports drink, and you'll play like Tom Brady.

So, why are Nike products so expensive? According to Megan Armstrong, a writer for Yahoo! Finance, Nike has had six of the largest *athletic endorsement compensation pack-ages in history.*[38] *They have had numerous multi-million dollar contracts with ath-*

Spending more on name brand clothes makes you a better athlete.

letes, including Tiger Woods, Michael Jordan, Cristine Ronaldo, Lebron James, Kobe Bryant, and Kevin Durant.[39] *LeBron James's current Nike compensation is estimated to be worth over $1 billion, while Kevin Durant signed a $300 million deal with a $50 million retirement package in 2014.*[40] *How can Nike afford to pay these athletes hundreds of millions in endorsement deals? It's because you and I, along with millions of other global customers, pay high prices for their products. Nike pays low, near impoverished wages to workers in third-world countries to manufacture its products and sells them significantly higher to pay their large endorsement contracts and other company costs.*

While in college, I learned a valuable lesson in understanding the difference between **wants and needs: Wants are basically more expensive versions of needs that provide little to no improvement***. I'm fortunate that I learned this lesson early in life and was able to deprogram myself from believing corporate marketing's hype before any financial damage was done." –Adam*

Okay, let's recap: You know the importance of setting goals, investing young, having a budget to be your financial roadmap, and

---

38.   Armstrong, Megan. "These 13 Athletes Won the Most Lucrative Endorsement Deals." Yahoo! Finance, February 24, 2020. https://finance.yahoo.com/news/13-athletes-won-most-lucrative-090000730.html.
39.   Ibid.
40.   Ibid.

you are on your way to obtaining or already have obtained a marketable career that pays well, has high employment prospects, and doesn't bury you in debt that prevents you from investing in your twenties. You are now on your way to becoming a money-printing machine. What's next? The next decision *is controlling your spending day after day,*

IMPORTANT!

It's not how much you make that matters, it's what you do with it.

month after month, and year after year by focusing on needs instead of wants—the fifth decision of the book. This decision is important because earning a good salary will have little impact on becoming a millionaire if you cannot control your spending. Thus, having the discipline to keep your spending under control that allows consistent investing should be a top priority.

Wants typically cost more than needs, and buying wants instead of needs reduces investment money. What's the point of having a good-paying job and low student loan debt if you can't control your spending and have nothing left to invest? *It's not how much you make that matters; it's what you do with it*. Life can be affordable. Life can be unaffordable. Life is more affordable when you buy your needs and less affordable when you buy your wants.

As we've reminded you at the start of every chapter, becoming a millionaire is a straightforward strategy with three primary inputs: *when you start, how much you invest, and what you invest in*. These inputs are in your control, and only you can make them happen. Decision 5: Buy Needs Instead of Wants, discusses how your spending choices affect how much you invest. If you don't want to be dumba$$, **buy needs instead of wants**.

WANTS VERSUS NEEDS

So, what's the difference? A need is something you must have to live, such as transportation, clothes, shoes, food, shelter, and water. A want is one of two things: It is either something that you can live without but still want, or it is a desire or something above and beyond what is needed to live, which includes transportation, clothes, shoes, food, shelter, and water. For example, an exotic vacation is something that you can live without. An $8 smoothie bought at your local gym is usually no better than a $1 smoothie that can be made at home.

OPERATION DON'T BE A DUMBA$$
Your Mission:
Focus on buying your needs versus your wants in order to invest as much money as possible.

It's important to point out a major difference between wants and needs: *Wants cost more—usually three to four times more.* For example, you *need* a pair of jeans, but you *want* a $120 pair of designer jeans instead of the $40 pair at Old Navy. You *need* transportation that safely and reliably gets you from point A to point B, but you *want* a 2023 Acura TL instead of a 2015 Toyota Camry. You *need* food, but you *want* organic produce from Whole Foods instead of getting roughly the same items at Lidl or Aldi. Each want does the same thing as a need but *costs significantly more to buy it*. Thus, *the main takeaway from this chapter is to focus on purchasing the more cost-effective needs, not the more expensive wants.* Doing this helps ensure you can still purchase items needed and invest.

Wants and needs are depreciable assets—they lose value over time—while investments appreciate—increase in value over time. For example, a TV is a depreciable asset. A new $2,000 TV will most likely be worth $500 or less in five years. So, it seems like common sense that spending all of your money on depreciable assets will not make you more prosperous

NOTE TO SELF

" Becoming a millionaire has less to do with how much you make and more about managing what you make. "

and certainly will not make you a millionaire. Instead, *focus on buying your needs or basic essentials and spend the rest on investments that appreciate.* Following this simple concept is an easy money-spending strategy to increase your chances of becoming a millionaire. Why do so many people struggle with wants versus needs? Why would someone spend $200 on a pair of Ray-Ban sunglasses when they could buy a similar-looking pair for $25 at Target? Why would someone lease a new car with a $500 monthly payment when they could buy a used car for $250 a month? Some don't even realize they are doing it because that's what they've always done, while others buy for a status symbol. Why buy an $8 smoothie at the gym after working out when you can wait fifteen

[FAKE NEWS]

Spending a lot of money on things makes people like you.

minutes and make one at home that costs you less than $1? It's disappointing that many people fall for the marketing trap: They need to buy expensive things or "wants" to impress people. If you live your life needing things, you will never make enough money. If you make $50,000, you'll need $75,000. If you make $500,000, you'll need $750,000. Becoming a millionaire has less to do with *how much* you make and more about *managing* what you make.

According to a 2022 CNBC survey, 36% of US employees who made $100,000 or more say they are living paycheck to paycheck.[41] To some, it may be mind-blowing that nearly one in three people who earn more than $100,000 a year can barely make ends meet. How can this happen? The answer is simple: wants. Cars, eating out, shopping, traveling, a large mortgage, you name it. All wants and immediate satisfaction while neglecting long-term wealth accumulation. How much you make means little, but what you do with your money means a lot. Someone who earns $100,000 with $100,000 taste is no different than someone who earns $50,000 with $50,000 taste or someone who earns one million dollars with one million dollar taste. It's all relative because none of them have any money left over for their future. Someone who makes $60,000 but invests $5,000 annually will be financially better off in the long run than someone who earns $1,000,000 but invests $0.

ARE THERE INSTANCES WHEN BUYING THE MORE EXPENSIVE ITEM IS A NEED?

Are there instances when buying the more expensive item *is* a need? Of course, there are. One great example is footwear. Buying a $125 pair of work shoes that increases comfortability and decreases the chances of blisters for those who spend many hours on their feet over

---

41.   Iacurci, Greg. "Amid High Inflation, 36% of Employees Earning $100,000 or More Say They Are Living Paycheck to Paycheck." CNBC, June 16, 2022. https://www.cnbc.com/2022/06/16/more-high-earners-are-living-paycheck-to-paycheck.html.

a $30 pair from Payless Shoes can certainly be seen as a need. Adam is an avid runner and always buys the higher brand footwear because they are lighter and fit better on his feet, improving his run time. However, it's important to note that not every expensive item is a need, and *the number of costly needs should be kept to a minimum.*

WHAT A DUMBA$$!

Latrell Sprewell, a former professional basketball player, and four-time NBA All-Star, made $100 million over his thirteen-year basketball career.[42] However, he may be more famous for what he said *off the court* than what he did *on the court*. In 2004, he rejected a three-year, $21 million contract because he said it wasn't enough to feed his family.[43] How can a $7 million a year salary not be enough to feed someone's family when an Extra Value Meal at McDonald's costs $7? The answer is simple: He blew all his money buying wants instead of his needs. Today, his net worth is estimated to be around $50,000, much less than the $100 million he made over his career.[44] He could have survived with two or three cars but wanted more. He could have survived with a nice speed boat but wanted a yacht. Every want was more expensive than his need, and he blew through a lot of money buying wants. If Sprewell had invested $500,000 a season or roughly 7% of his entire NBA earnings while playing and did whatever he wanted with the rest, then he would have retired in 2005 with $13,076,057. By 2021, his net worth would

42.   Greder, Andy. "Ex-Timberwolves Star Latrell Sprewell Pokes Fun at Broke Self." *Twin Cities Pioneer Press*, October 24, 2018. https://www.twincities.com/2016/02/10/timberwolves-latrell-sprewells-version-of-success-a-tv-commercial/.
43.   Norris, Luke. "What Happened to Former NBA Star Latrell Sprewell?" *Sportscasting*, March 22, 2020. https://www.sportscasting.com/what-happened-to-former-nba-star-latrell-sprewell/.
44.   Ibid.

have increased to \$44,797,821, which is slightly less than half of his total career earnings.

Latrell Sprewell is not the only professional athlete with wants-versus-needs problems. According to Sports Illustrated, 78% of NFL players are broke within two years of retiring.[45] This is because they probably bought too many wants instead of needs and neglected to invest.

DID YOU KNOW?

If someone had invested \$410 each year since Latrell Sprewell joined the NBA and earned an 8% annual return, he or she would have more money today than Latrell Sprewell, who made \$100 million over that same time period.

TIME FOR SELF-REFLECTION

Think about the things that you buy for a second. How many purchases do you *need*? How many do you *want*? Some people spend because they unknowingly have been programmed by corporate marketing to spend every penny and don't know any better. Others may spend because of

> " Once you really accept that spending money doesn't equal happiness, you have half the battle won.
> –Ernest Callenbach "

---

45.   Torre, Pablo S. "How (and Why) Athletes Go Broke." Sports Illustrated Vault, March 23, 2009. https://vault.si.com/vault/2009/03/23/how-and-why-athletes-go-broke.

societal pressures and a need to keep up with others and don't want to be different.

For those of you who feel like there are societal pressures to keep up with others, please consider the following question, "Did the clothes or the bicycle you rode in kindergarten impact who you are today, who your friends are, or what accomplishments you achieved?" Most likely, the answer is "no" because why would anyone today care what you wore or rode in kindergarten? Your accomplishments and friends are most likely with you because of

What does buying all the expensive stuff really get me?

POINT TO PONDER

who you are and not what you owned. What you owned along the way had little impact on your outcome. In other words, the items you had as a kid or ten years ago had little to no impact on where or who you are now. *Why would you think what you buy today will impact where you are in another ten years*? Again, it most likely won't. In another ten years, your car and clothes will have little impact on who you become. However, what will matter is how much money you have in ten, twenty, or thirty years, and a good way to get there is to limit your expensive wants and instead focus on your more cost-effective needs. What's ironic is that yesterday's "cool kids" who overbought the nice things are today's "living paycheck to paycheck adults," and the "uncool kids" who didn't buy the expensive stuff are now "the millionaires." Time changes things.

"A MINI LATRELL SPREWELL"

You don't have to be a professional athlete to blow all your money on wants or things above and beyond what you need. It can happen to anyone, anytime, anywhere. One of Adam's Air Force ROTC classmates became a maintenance officer after college and later told Adam a very prevalent story for this chapter: One day, Adam's friend came to work and noticed a decked-out, beautiful, brand new pick-up truck that likely cost at least $60,000 parked by the office. He thought the truck belonged to a senior Air Force officer whose annual salary exceeds $130,000 a year. However, to his surprise, it belonged to a young, enlisted member who lived in an on-base government-provided dorm room and, excluding his housing allowance, earned approximately $23,000 a year. He later found out that the young enlisted member had to pay roughly $0.80 for every $1.00 to pay the truck payment, which didn't include insurance or gas. Factoring in gas and insurance, this young enlisted member paid nearly every penny that he made to drive this truck. How was he going to buy food? Or anything for that matter? How was he going to invest? This young enlisted service member was a dumba$$—plain and simple. He *needed* a vehicle to get him from point A to point B safely. However, he overspent on what he *wanted* and, as a result, destroyed any

> **"**
>
> I love money. I love everything about it. I bought some pretty good stuff. Got me a $300 pair of socks. Got a fur sink. An electric dog polisher. A gasoline-powered turtleneck sweater. And, of course, I bought some dumb stuff, too.
> -Steve Martin
>
> **"**

chances of investing young and, most likely, severely impacted his financial future. It seems like common sense, but you have to invest if you want to be a millionaire, and you can't be one if you spend all your money on dumb stuff.

THINK OF YOUR WANTS AND NEEDS LIKE FILLING UP YOUR TANK OF GAS

We live down the street from a gas station called the Express Shop, which sells some of the cheapest gas in the area. This station's gas prices are usually $0.20 to $0.25 less per gallon than the other gas stations. Because the gas is less expensive, it is always busy. Always. The line is constantly out on the main road, often blocking traffic. Many of you may have seen similar long lines at a local Costco or Sam's Club gas station, which sells gas at a discounted rate.

OPERATION DON'T BE A DUMBA$$
Your Mission:
Buy your desired product for its intended purpose at the lowest price.

We estimate that customers wait in line for thirty minutes to save $0.20 to $0.25 on a gallon of gas. To put the savings into perspective, a $0.25 savings per gallon on a twenty-gallon tank equates to *a total savings of $5.00*. $5.00. In other words, for less than the price of an Extra

Value Meal at McDonald's, customers are willing to wait in line for thirty minutes. Interestingly, few seem to care about the brand name when getting gas for a car. Whether it's Exxon Mobil, Shell, Chevron, Sunoco, the Express Shop, or any other brand, *gas is gas,* and *most customers only care about getting the cheapest gas.* Yet, excluding gas, many of these same customers buy brand-name products when buying other items. For example, judging by the number of cars seen in parking lots, few apply this frugality concept to groceries. For example, a dozen eggs at Lidl, an east coast discount grocery store, costs less than $1 but almost $3.50 at other grocery stores.

Why do some people not care about the brand of gas and spend thirty minutes waiting in line to save $5 in gas but drive more expensive brand-name cars, which are clearly above and beyond what is needed to get from point A to point B and costs *hundreds of extra dollars* a month? Or many of the same customers shop at non-discount grocery stores, which likely costs them *hundreds of extra dollars* a month for roughly the same groceries?

NOTE TO SELF

" It's nearly impossible to become a millionaire if I spend every dollar that I earn. "

Let's take this gas lesson and apply it to the rest of your spending. We want you to think of most of your purchases like a tank of gas: For most situations, *buy your desired product for its intended purpose at the lowest price possible, and ignore the brand name.* There is almost always a less expensive option for nearly everything you buy.

THE 'BIG 6' WANTS VERSUS NEEDS: THE PRIMARY THINGS YOU WILL SPEND MONEY ON

When it comes to spending, you have 100% control over what you spend your money on. Sure, your car breaks down every now and then, or you have an unforeseen event, but you have 100% control over what you do with your money. If you want to invest but do not have enough money, *change your lifestyle by spending your money differently.* While this is an obvious statement, someone earning $50,000 a year can invest by making smart lifestyle and spending decisions just as easily as someone earning $150,000 a year. How do *we* know that? Because after college, both of us made less than $50,000, and through good decisions, we invested because we monitored our spending and didn't have any college debt holding us back. Remember, *it's not how much you make; it's what you do with your money that matters.*

> **NOTE TO SELF**
> " If you don't have enough money to invest, change your lifestyle by spending your money differently. "

We will not lecture you on how to spend your money, but we want to point out that you should be consciously aware. Below are what we call The Big 6. These six items have the biggest impact on your spending, and we wanted to provide some advice on how to be successful.

WANTS VS. NEEDS

THE BIG 6 PEOPLE SPEND THEIR MONEY ON

WHERE YOU LIVE:

Typically your highest expense.

Rent the lowest-priced, acceptable unit because a few hundred difference makes a substantial difference in your monthly budget.

EATING OUT

It is almost always less expensive to cook at home instead of eating out. In most cases it is three to four times less expensive.

Buy a crock pot, air fryer, or other appliance that saves time.

VACATIONS:

Vacations can be costly. Flights, lodging, and eating out add up quickly.

Explore cost-saving alternatives: Drive rather than fly. Look for deals. Pack a lunch on travel days. Travel on less-traveled days, or travel during non-peak season. Travel to areas with family or friends.

Start a vacation fund and put in a small amount each month.

GROCERY SHOPPING:

Shop at discount stores such as Aldi and Lidl or bulk discount stores.

Use coupons when available.

Join any shoppers club.

CARS

Buy a used, reliable vehicle such as a Toyota or Honda.

Buy instead of leasing. Leasing ensures you will always have a car payment, which you want to avoid.

Drive your paid-off car as long as it's safe to drive.

BUYING "STUFF"

Follow your budget on what you can afford and only buy what you can pay off at the end of the month.

Buy used when you can.

Wait for sales (Black Friday).

Ask yourself, "Do I really need this and is there a more cost-effective alternative?"

CAN I AFFORD IT?

The *Suze Orman Show* was one of our favorite money management shows because Suze spends a good portion of her show talking about money management, especially spending. If you are new to money management, we recommend watching some of her shows. Each show has a segment called "Can I Afford It?" where a caller asks Suze if they can afford something they want to buy.

NEEDS VS. WANTS

You don't need to eat out, you want to.
You don't need the larger apartment, you want it.
You don't need a costly vacation, you want it.
You don't need an expensive new car, you want it.
You don't need to shop at Whole Foods, you want to.

Before Suze gives the caller her answer, she asks them to "show her the money." The caller then provides Suze with their age, monthly income, monthly expenses, debt, savings, liquid money or money that can turn into cash quickly, and retirement amount. Suze then assesses the caller's financial situation and either approves or denies the caller's purchase and provides her rationale. This reflective process is vital for anyone who wants to make large purchases. Pausing and asking yourself, "Can I afford it?" and many times, "Do I really need it, or can I get by with another lower-cost alternative?" will significantly affect your spending habits. Training yourself early to make consistent and smart spending choices regarding your wants versus your needs is essential. Having the awareness and discipline to tell yourself, "No, I can't afford it," or, "No, I don't need it, or I can buy something else at a lower price," is an important skill to learn. *What you don't buy is often more important than what you buy.*

SECOND- AND THIRD-ORDER EFFECTS

When it comes to your spending decisions, there are always financial consequences, or what we like to call second- and third-order effects. Or in other words, what happens after something occurs and what happens after that. For example, buying a new phone (action) results in a higher monthly payment (second-order effect)

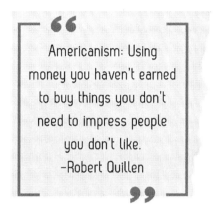

> **"**
> Americanism: Using money you haven't earned to buy things you don't need to impress people you don't like.
> –Robert Quillen
> **"**

and decreases your investment income (third-order effect). Likewise, suppose someone has a poor diet and exercise habits. In that case, their second-order effects are becoming overweight, and their third-order effect is having a higher chance of dying at a younger age. Another example is attending a costly university and attaining a major with low prospects of getting a job or a low salary. The second-order effect is higher student loan payments, and the third-order effect is less money to invest young and a lower chance of becoming a millionaire.

Understanding this concept is important as you embark on your future. The financial consequence of overspending $25 here and $50 there may not always be immediate or even within the next year, but *these spending decisions have significant impacts over your lifetime.* Unfortunately, this is the problem with spending, and we frequently fail to see the long-term effects of our decisions. It's not until later in life that one day that some people scratch their heads and wonder why they don't have as much money as they had hoped. While there could be many reasons, a big reason is spending too much on stuff they didn't need rather than investing.

WANTS VERSUS NEEDS IN REAL LIFE

Okay, you get the point. Spend wisely. Think about your spending decisions and evaluate your needs versus your wants. Let's look at an example, buying a car, and see how it impacts your future. You *want* a new one, but, again, you only *need* a car that safely and reliably gets you from point A to point B. So here are your two options:

Option 1: Buy a new car for $33,000 that costs $550 a month with a five-year loan.

Option 2: Buy a seven-year-old, used, reliable car with 70,000 miles for $15,000 that costs $250 a month with a five-year loan and invest the $300 monthly savings from not buying a new car in an S&P 500 Index Fund.

What are the second and third-order effects of these decisions at age sixty and seventy if you do Option 2 at age nineteen and twenty-three? The second-order effect for Option 2 is having an extra $300 to invest, and the third-order effect is shown in Table 22 below:

	Amount of Money at Age 60 and 70	
Car-Buying Age	**Age 60**	**Age 70**
After High School (Age 19)	$393,361	$849,238
After College (Age 23)	$289,132	$624,215

Table 22. Second- and Third-Order Effects of Buying a New Versus Used Car

Buying a used (need) car instead of a new (want) car and investing the $300 monthly difference over five years increased your future net worth by somewhere between a quarter of a million dollars to approximately $400,000 at age sixty and almost twice as much more at seventy. In both options, you purchased a car that gets you from point A to point B and does its intended purpose, but *one also makes you a lot richer than the other*. So, Option 1 gets you a car, and Option 2 gets you a car and $289,132 at age sixty if you bought it at age twenty-three. By focusing on your needs instead of wants, you will be able to buy *ten new cars* if you bought the used one after high school.

What does this example demonstrate? If you want to be a millionaire, we strongly suggest *never buying a new car (want) in your teens and twenties. Instead, buy a reliable, used car (need) and drive it as long as possible to avoid making car payments.* Thirty years from now, you won't even remember why you wanted that new car so badly, but you'll surely miss the money you didn't make on the investment difference.

You may be thinking, "Well, yeah, a $300 monthly car payment makes a big difference, but saving $20 by cooking at home versus eating out is not a big deal," or, "Who cares if I shop at Whole Foods?" These small instances, or what we like to call "the millionaire death by 1,000 cuts," make a *huge* difference. Small decisions like these on your wants versus needs happen multiple times, every day of the week. A $5-Starbucks here and a $15-going-out-with-your-friends lunch there. They all add up. Many people are often oblivious to the fact that they are doing it. How much do small, frequent wants versus needs decisions *really cost you*? Let's say you make several small changes and save $100. For example, your friends are out of town this week, and you cook at your apartment all week instead of going out your usual three times. Since you spent less, you decide to invest your $100 savings. Table 23 shows how much more money you will have at sixty and seventy if you save and invest $100 at different ages.

Age	Savings	Value at 60	Value at 70
16	$100	$2,956	$6,381
17	$100	$2,737	$5,908
18	$100	$2,534	$5,471
19	$100	$2,346	$5,065
20	$100	$2,172	$4,690
21	$100	$2,012	$4,343
22	$100	$1,863	$4,021
23	$100	$1,725	$3,723
24	$100	$1,597	$3,447

Table 23: Saving and Investing $100 and Its Value at Age Sixty and Seventy

So, based on several smaller decisions, a simple $100 savings at age sixteen that is instead invested will turn into about $2,956 at age sixty and $6,381 by age seventy.

Next week, you save and invest another $100, which adds another $2,956 at age sixty. After two weeks, you have saved and invested $200 and have added $5,912 to your future net worth at age sixty. *After four weeks of saving $400, you have increased your future net worth at age sixty by $11,824.* You begin to connect the dots on how saving a few dollars here and there adds up and turns into a lot of money later in life. Slowly, you begin to make a few small spending changes here and there, and before you know it, saving money is now second nature. Instead of viewing it as $100 in the present, you now view it as a future $2,956 if you are sixteen or $2,534 if you are eighteen.

NOTE TO SELF

Be 'cheap' when buying stuff and spend frivolously on investments.

While saving money used to be considered impossible, it is now as normal, natural, and automatic as getting into your car and driving to school or work. Each pay period, you are now making smart spending decisions that save a few hundred dollars which will turn into *ten thousand dollars* later in life. You continue making smart spending decisions that save a few hundred dollars a paycheck for a year, which will turn into a *hundred* thousand dollars later in life. Continuing this behavior consistently throughout your teens and twenties will turn into a *million* dollars *or more*. Once a dumba$$ who spent every penny of your paycheck, you have now turned into a money-making machine by simply making better spending decisions and buying cost-effective alternatives.

What does this prove? It proves that multiple, minor lifestyle adjustments in your teens and twenties will have significant financial implications later in life. The younger you adjust and invest, the more it is worth. How much is your financial future altered by the clothes you wear? The food you buy? The place you live? Your

FUN FACT:
Adam's grandmother paid for her entire vacation to Norway on grocery rebates alone.

college debt? Vacations? This section's main takeaway is *your day-to-day spending choices will result in a possible loss or gain of millions of dollars to your future net worth.* No matter your income or age, everyone can cut back on spending by buying needs versus wants.

APPLYING NEEDS VERSUS WANTS TO AN EARLIER EXAMPLE

Next, let's apply the concept of needs versus wants to an earlier example. Let's revisit John from the budgeting chapter and his budget in Table 11. If you recall, John had a monthly budget deficit of $900; he spent $900 more than he earned every month. However, John decides to adjust his lifestyle and spending budget and reevaluates his needs versus his wants to improve his finances before it's too late.

IMPORTANT!

Your day-to-day spending choices will result in a possible gain or loss of millions of dollars to your future net worth.

What changes did he make? First, he moves into a shared apartment, dropping his rent from $1,000 a month to $700. Second, after his car lease ends, he buys a good-conditioned, eight-year-old Toyota Camry, costing $250 a month. John realizes that buying and driving a paid-off car allows him to eventually not have a car payment, whereas leasing ensures that he always has a several-hundred-dollar car payment, which means less investment money. He also decides to continue using his current iPhone instead of upgrading to the newest one once it is paid off, therefore paying $75 a month instead of $150. His iPhone still works after it's paid off, so what does the newest iPhone get him other than more expenses? Third, he and his roommate set their thermostat a few degrees lower in the winter and a few degrees higher in the summer to save on utility bills. In addition, they also open their windows at night in the early summer and fall to cool the apartment down without running the air conditioner, which further reduces his utility bills. As a result, his average monthly electric bill is split two ways and drops from \$125 to \$50 a month, his average gas bill drops from \$50 to \$20 a month, and cable drops to \$50.

John also begins shopping at his local Aldi and Lidl grocery stores. He is shocked at how much lower his grocery bill is for the same products. The Digiorno Self-Rising Crust pizza that John loves to eat used to cost him \$7.00 at his local grocery store, but buying the Lidl brand Self-Rising Crust pizza now costs \$3.25. John can still get the pizzas, eggs, milk, meat, chips, and everything he got at his old grocery store but for a reduced price. As a result, he saves 25% on his grocery bill, decreasing from \$200 to \$150 twice a month, or \$100 monthly savings. Finally, John lowers his spending budget from \$800 to \$650 and decides to go out with his friends two nights a week instead of three nights a week and eats out twice a week instead of four times. John's old budget from Chapter 3 and his updated Budget from this chapter (Chapter 5) are put together side by side in Table 24 for comparison.

First Half of the Month	Chapter 3	Chapter 5	Second Half of the Month	Chapter 3	Chapter 5
Paycheck	\$ 2,000.00	\$2,000.00	Paycheck	\$2,000.00	\$2,000.00
Expenses			Expenses		
S&P500 Index Investment	\$ 300.00	\$ 300.00	Groceries	\$ 200.00	\$ 150.00
Rent	\$ 1,000.00	\$ 700.00	Gasoline	\$ 50.00	\$ 50.00
Car Payment	\$ 400.00	\$ 250.00	Spending	\$ 800.00	\$ 650.00
Cell Phone	\$ 150.00	\$ 75.00	Total Expenses	\$1,050.00	\$ 850.00
Cable/Internet	\$ 75.00	\$ 50.00			
Utilities (Electric)	\$ 125.00	\$ 50.00			
Utilities (Gas)	\$ 50.00	\$ 20.00			
Gym Membership	\$ 100.00	\$ 100.00			
College Loan Payment	\$ 600.00	\$ 600.00			
Gasoline	\$ 50.00	\$ 50.00			
Groceries	\$ 200.00	\$ 150.00			
Spending	\$ 800.00	\$ 650.00			
Total Expenses	\$ 3,850.00	\$2,995.00			
Remaining Funds	\$(1,850.00)	\$ (995.00)	Remaining Funds	\$ 950.00	\$1,150.00
			Monthly Remaining Funds	\$ (900.00)	\$ 155.00

Table 24. John's Updated Budget

John focused on needs instead of wants, and these decisions are reflected in his updated budget above. How much do these lifestyle changes

You have to spend a lot of money to have fun.

save him? *Rather than having a $900 deficit, he now has a $155 surplus,* or $155 more than what he needs. With this surplus, John then decides to invest an additional $75 a month and put $80 into his emergency fund. By focusing on needs instead of wants, John has turned his financial fortunes around with a monthly change of $1,055 and is well on his way to becoming a millionaire.

What is the main takeaway? There are *always* ways to cut spending from your budget to turn your budget around. And, if you can't find something, you are not looking hard enough.

KEY TAKEAWAYS OF DECISION 5:

- Wants are more expensive versions of needs
- From groceries to lattes to cars—there are always cost-effective alternatives
- Your everyday spending decisions can result in a loss or gain of millions of dollars over your lifetime

To conclude, every choice you make is precisely that: your choice. You decide how to spend your money, where to go to school, what to major in, and where to work. These choices relate to money, financial awareness, and needs versus wants. Excluding extenuating circumstances, you control how you spend your money. *What you drive, what you wear, or what you own does not define who you are.* By making smart day-to-day financial decisions in your teens and twenties, you will be rewarded with a lot of money to buy the nicer things you always wanted—the fancy car, the perfect lake house, or the extravagant European vacation. It's tempting to spend money immediately, but investing gives you a greater return. Give up the dress now for a vacation to Greece in twenty years.

To be a millionaire, having the discipline to control your spending is an absolute must-have skill. Buying your needs instead of wants is an easy rule to help control spending. It all comes down to delaying gratification. It all comes down to how you manage your expenses. It all comes down to you and your spending choices. We know this stuff doesn't sound fun and exciting

NOTE TO SELF

"You are not defined by the car you drive, the clothes you wear, or what you own."

and easy and that denying instant gratification is not as cool as a Tik Tok video. But, managing wants versus needs in combination with a marketable career while investing young with a budget guiding you will make you unstoppable. This is the winning ticket when it comes to becoming a millionaire.

Now, the question is, "What should you do with your investment money?"

DECISION 6:
INVEST IN AN S&P
500 INDEX FUND

"Investing should be more like watching paint dry or watching grass grow. If you want excitement, take $800 and go to Las Vegas."
-Paul Samuelson

"Before I primarily **invested in S&P 500 Index Funds**, I invested in individual stocks. As you know, I lived in Vegas during my first Air Force assignment and was there during the 2008–09 Great Recession, which had the biggest stock market declines in my life. Vegas's economy was hit especially hard. Before the recession, the Vegas Strip was always crowded. It didn't matter what day it was; it was always busy. A year later, I could walk the strip on the weekends, and it was almost a ghost town. Throughout the city, neighborhoods were littered with abandoned houses with foreclosure signs out front. Some neighborhoods appeared to be small, empty ghost towns. It was strange.

The Venetian, my favorite Vegas casino, is owned by Las Vegas Sands and is a publicly-traded stock, meaning that you, me, or anyone can buy shares or ownership of the company. During the 2008–09 Great Recession, all Vegas casino stocks were crushed and down 95%+: Las Vegas Sands, Wynn, MGM... all of them. Las Vegas Sands stock had been trading for over $100 a share, or how much it costs to own a share of the company, just the year before, and by early March 2009 was trading less than $0.60 a share. I had $8,000 in my stock brokerage account and planned on putting in an order for $8,000 worth of Las Vegas Sands shares. I had a good feeling that the casino stocks would recover. After all, it was Vegas, a highly desired, international vacation destination.

My rationale was simple: People will always want to get away and party in Vegas. However, I made the mistake of asking for advice from a professional, my dad, who had been a stockbroker earlier in his career. I told him I wanted to put $8,000 into Las Vegas Sands, to which he told me that I was crazy to do so. Listening to my dad, whose advice I usually followed, I never submitted the buy order. By September 2010, Las Vegas Sands had rebounded from less than $0.60 to over $45 a share. My $8,000 investment would have been worth around $654,000 in less than eighteen months and would have been enough for my Buffalo County hunting land.

*Thus, from an early age, I learned a costly, important lesson: No one, not even highly educated investment professionals, knows what is going to happen in the market consistently, and nearly all investment professionals underperform the S&P 500 Index in the long run. Therefore, **thinking that you or an investment professional will outperform the S&P 500 Index over twenty or more years may be the biggest misconception in all of investing and money management.** Yet, unfortunately, it continues to be believed over and over again.*

*I'll admit, at first it was hard coming to this realization. Along with many other investors, I started out thinking that I was smarter than the broad market and could outperform the market by wisely picking individual stocks myself. If not me, then certainly investment money management professionals, who are much 'smarter' than everyone else, must have higher returns over the long run. A licensed plumber, nurse, or electrician is most likely better at their job than you or I would be, so an investment professional must be better as well… right? However, after a lot of reading, coming to grips with reality, and **setting my ego aside**, I realized that neither I nor nearly any investment professional could outperform*

*the S&P 500 Index in the long run; **trying to do so is, was, and
forever will be, a losing and expensive investment strategy.** Most
investors come to a similar realization at some point, but only after
underperforming the S&P 500 Index by tens or even hundreds of
thousands of dollars. So, I switched my investment strategy and
now heavily invest in low-cost S&P 500 Index Funds to save myself
hundreds of thousands of dollars in underperformance and from
paying substantially higher fees. Save yourself the trouble and
underperformance and invest in low-cost S&P 500 Index Funds
right away. As dull as an S&P 500 Index Fund may be, **nothing
is boring about their long-term performance against investment
professionals.**" –Adam*

You have made it to the final decision: investing in S&P 500
Index Funds. You have chosen to make becoming a millionaire your
goal, invest young, stick to a budget, obtain a marketable career with as
little debt as possible, and control your spending by focusing on needs
instead of wants. These decisions have gotten you to this moment: You
are ready to invest.

For the last time, becoming a millionaire is a straightforward
strategy that is a function of three primary inputs: *when you start,
how much you invest, and what you invest in.* These inputs are in your
control, and only you can make them happen. So, this final chapter is all
about what you invest in.

Now is the point in the book when you learn how to turn all that
hard-earned money into millions. Now is the fun part. Now is when
you have long-term determination to see your plan through. Now is
when you start investing.

What are you going to invest in? Bitcoin? Options? The "next"
Amazon? Nope, you're going to invest in *an S&P 500 Index Fund.* Huh?

Index Funds? But why? "I heard my friend's older brother made a lot of money investing in _____ (fill in the most current investing fad)." *Because index funds are where you get the most bang for your buck.* They are easy to invest in and manage, you don't have to get lucky and "guess" the right investment, you don't have to hire anyone to do the work for you, the fees are low, and most

NOTE TO SELF

It's time to make my money work for me.

importantly, they *outperform other equities in the long run.* They're also attractive because you don't have to read the Wall Street Journal every day or closely monitor individual stocks, taking time away from things you enjoy doing. Basically, you put your money in, and the capitalistic system does "the work" for you.

Now is when you let your money work for you instead of you working for your money. One day, your investments will make more money for you in one year than by working forty-hour weeks. How soon that day arrives depends on how early you start and how much you invest.

Please note that throughout this chapter, we sometimes refer to the S&P 500 Index as "the market"; however, the market and the S&P 500 Index are the same thing.

RISK/REWARD

First off, let's discuss investment risk and reward. Risk is the amount of uncertainty, while the reward is the amount of benefit gained. In investing, risk and reward go together. The higher the risk, the higher the potential reward or return on investment, and the higher the risk of losing your investment. Meanwhile, the lower the risk, the lower the potential reward or return on investment, and the lower the risk of losing your investment. For example, putting money in a savings account is considered low-risk because the Federal Deposit Insurance Corporation ensures all accounts up to $250,000, and the chance of losing your money is minimal. Thus, a savings account typically has a lower return than other investments because of its low-risk level.

> **66**
> How many millionaires do you know who have become wealthy by investing in a savings account?
> I rest my case.
> –Robert G. Allen
> **99**

Meanwhile, stocks or equities are considered high-risk and high return because of their ability to lose or gain money. As a young investor, you want risk. The S&P 500 Index Fund has all stock exposure, but its risk is lower than owning individual stocks because it comprises 500 individual companies' stocks and not just one. Thus, *an S&P 500 Index Fund has an adequate risk/reward ratio for a young investor—not too risky but not too conservative.*

IS AN 8% ANNUAL RETURN TOO OPTIMISTIC?

The S&P 500 Index has averaged roughly an 8% return since its inception, and an 8% annual return has been used for calculations in this book. However, the S&P 500 Index has gone through periods of little to even negative returns and other periods of high returns. For example, from March 1928 to March 1941 (thirteen years), the S&P 500 had an annual return of 0.66% with dividends (a company's profits paid out in cash to a stock's shareholder) reinvested.[46] Meanwhile, from March 1982 to March 2022 (forty years), the S&P 500 Index had an average return of 12.17%, with dividends reinvested.[47] Thus, you will experience periods where the annual return is less than 8% and will experience periods where the annual return is greater than 8%. However, it's essential to have a long-term perspective and stay focused during lackluster periods of return.

TRUST-A SACRED BOND

We understand that many of you might have difficulty trusting anyone or any system with your hard-earned money. Which company do you choose? Whose advice do you take? What if you lose all your hard-earned money? You have every right to be skeptical of what you hear. "Invest in this, invest in that. I have a great investment tip… My friend made a lot of money in this…" We've heard it all. What is fact? What isn't? Who can you trust? Who can't you trust? Many times, you can't trust investment professionals because they have their own financial interests involved in their decision-making. Many investment professionals receive a commission on selling you a certain financial product that may or may not be in your best interest. But they wear a nice suit and talk like they know

NOTE TO SELF
" Invest in an S&P 500 Index Fund. "

---

46.   PK, "S&P 500 Return Calculator, with Dividend Reinvestment." DQYDJ, July 7, 2022. https://dqydj.com/sp-500-return-calculator/.
47.   Ibid.

what they're talking about, and so you trust them with your money. Be aware that many times, financial professionals may be more interested *in their financial interests than yours.*

S&P 500 Index Funds are great investments for those with trust issues. Why? Because as an S&P 500 Index Fund owner, you are an owner of all of the 500 largest American companies. You'll have ownership in Amazon, McDonald's, Home Depot, Nike, Starbucks, Apple, and the other 494 largest American companies. Each company's CEO works long hours, day after day, doing everything possible to maximize the stock's return for you, the shareholder. When you are an S&P 500 Index Fund owner, the companies are working for *you*, doing everything possible to make *you rich*. A company's goal is to maximize profits and return value to its shareholders, so having ownership in the company means *their interests* are *your interests.*

WHY CHOOSE INDEX FUNDS OVER ACTIVELY MANAGED MUTUAL FUNDS?

Mutual funds are a common investment. There are two kinds of mutual funds—active mutual funds and passive, commonly known as index funds (the one we want you to invest in). Fund managers manage both types of mutual funds. However, an actively managed fund is managed by a *full-time fund manager and a team of specialists* who buy and sell stocks that they believe will maximize the fund's return. Meanwhile, a passive fund or an index fund (again, what we want you to invest in) is managed by a *part-time fund manager* who balances the fund on a semi-regular basis to match the composition of the fund's index or benchmark or what it is compared against. For example, an S&P 500 Index Fund models the composition of the S&P 500 Index.

In other words, an actively managed mutual fund is run by a full-time team of investment professionals, while an index fund is not.

Why are we discussing the difference between an index fund and an actively managed mutual fund? Because a mutual fund's fees, or how much you pay someone to manage it, vary drastically between the two types. These fees cover operating expenses, including salaries and overhead (ongoing costs required to run a business). This matters because actively managed funds' fees are substantially higher than that of index funds. For example, most active mutual funds charge at least an annual fee of 0.7% or higher on the amount invested. In other words, the fund charges $7 each year for every $1,000 invested, which comes out to 0.7%.

Meanwhile, index funds charge a fraction of what active funds charge. For example, Vanguard's 500 Index Admiral Fund charges 0.04%. This means that the fund charges $0.40 each year for every $1,000 invested. While the difference between paying $7 a year per thousand (0.7%) and $0.40 a year per thousand (0.04%) may

IMPORTANT!

Most investment professionals underperform the market in the long run and charge you a lot of money.

seem like a small difference, it makes *a substantial difference over the long run*. In addition, these fees are charged every year. When your balance increases, so too do the fees. Thus, a $1,000,000 account invested in a fund with a 0.7% annual fee charges $7,000 annually. It's also important to note that *these fees are paid regardless of fund performance*. Whether the fund has a 50% annual return or a 35% annual loss, the fund still charges the fees.

You're probably a little stunned that we would recommend investing in an index fund over an investment managed by professionals. After all, professionals are supposed to be better at their field of expertise than non-professionals. So, why don't we want an investment professional handling your investments? Because, to let you in on a secret, most investment professionals *underperform or have a lower annual return than an S&P 500 Index Fund over the long run and charge their clients a lot of money to underperform.*[48] In other words, more money for them, less money for you. Shouldn't it be *more money* for you since you're paying them to do so?

How do we know this? Well, let's take a closer look. First, according to a recent CNBC survey, what percent of actively managed large-cap (companies with a market cap of $10 billion or more) mutual funds (managed by professionals) beat the S&P 500 Index (not managed by professionals) over ten years? What do you think? Is it 50%? 70%? 80%? Higher? Nope, not even close. The answer is *10%*.[49] Think about that for a second. *Over ten years, only 10% of actively managed large-cap mutual funds managed by highly educated investment professionals beat the S&P 500 Index.* Or in other words, 90% of investment professionals <u>did not</u> beat the S&P 500 index over ten years. In addition, active fund managers can easily charge about twenty-one times or more than an index fund manager

> **NOTE TO SELF**
> "Over ten years, only 10% of actively managed large cap mutual funds beat the S&P 500 Index"

---

48.   Carrel, Lawrence. "Passive Management Marks Decade of Beating Active U.S. Stock Funds." Forbes, April 20, 2020. https://www.forbes.com/sites/lcarrel/2020/04/20/passive-beats-active-large-cap-funds-10-years-in-a-row/?sh=3d4b48e047b0.
49.   Ibid.

to *underperform*. Basically, if you invest in an actively managed fund, you are paying someone twenty-one times or more than what it costs to invest in an S&P 500 Index Fund to most likely make you less money.

While actively managed mutual funds can struggle to beat the S&P 500 Index over ten years, they can also have a hard time outperforming its benchmark over an even shorter time depending on the year. For example, in 2021, 80% of all actively managed US stock mutual funds underperformed their benchmark.[50] Or said in another way, only 20% of investing professionals beat their benchmark *in one year.*

So why do people still invest in actively managed funds? Mainly because most don't even know what an index fund is, let alone are aware of how bad

Paying a professional to manage my money will make me more money than investing in an S&P 500 Index in the long run.

professional money managers are at their job. It's not like it is headline news. Investing is an area that many people think is too complicated, and they hire a professional as they would for home or automotive needs. When, in actuality, *investing may be the only profession where hiring a professional is worse than not using one.* This seems counterintuitive, but that's what the facts say.

What are we trying to tell you? *The biggest scam in the investment industry is that investment professionals beat the S&P 500 Index in the long run, but they don't.*

Suppose you ignore this essential tip and decide to invest in an active fund. In that case, you have a 90% chance of underperforming

50.   Iacurci, Greg. "Odds Are, You're Better off Buying an Index Fund. Here's Why." CNBC, March 21, 2022. https://www.cnbc.com/2022/03/21/why-index-funds-are-often-a-better-bet-than-active-funds.html.

the S&P 500 Index over ten years and likely near a 100% chance of underperforming it over a twenty-, thirty-, or forty-year period, which will cost you *hundreds of thousands of dollars.* Investing in actively managed funds means underperforming and paying higher fees, which results in *a lot less money for you.*

Jack Boyle, the founder of index funds, knew the challenges of beating the market in the long run by picking individual stocks and how high-cost mutual fund managers had a track record of underperforming the S&P 500 Index. From that, he created the low-cost index fund and famously stated, "Don't look for the needle in the haystack. Just buy the haystack."[51] In other words, don't try to pick "the one" of a thousand stocks; instead, buy all of them by investing in an S&P500 Index Fund. Of course, investing in low-cost S&P 500 Index Funds may not be as exciting as other investments. Talking about your S&P 500 Index Fund is usually not the center of conversation when discussing investments at a BBQ or other social gatherings, but that's okay. Over the long run, your S&P 500 Index Fund will likely outperform others, and you'll have more money than they do.

DID YOU KNOW?

In 2007, Warren Buffet bet one million dollars that an S&P 500 Index Fund would outperform hedge funds over a ten-year period. The index fund gained 125.8% while the five hedge funds average gain was 36%. Buffet won the bet.

51.　"A Quote from the Little Book of Common Sense Investing." Goodreads, accessed May 17, 2022. https://www.goodreads.com/quotes/920319-don-t-look-for-the-needle-in-the-haystack-just-buy.

HOW MUTUAL FUND RESEARCH CAN BE MISLEADING

Some of you may be interested in researching mutual funds and investing in funds in addition to the S&P 500 Index. If so, we'd like to briefly discuss how mutual fund research can be misleading and how to avoid falling into the mutual fund investment trap: a company's funds outperform the S&P 500 Index. First, *it's important to note that most mutual fund companies display their fund's performance before fees.* So, the mutual fund companies are not being 100% honest with you. In addition, a fund's performance against the S&P 500 Index will change after factoring in fees.

To prove our point, let's examine one popular mutual fund company, Vanguard, and their stock mutual funds with an account minimum of less than $50,000 to open and compare its performance against the S&P 500 Index. At the time of this book's writing, Vanguard's funds were filtered and found that they have forty stock mutual funds with an account minimum of less than $50,000 and have been around for ten years.[52] Vanguard's forty mutual funds' ten-year return were then arranged from highest to lowest to see how each did against the S&P 500 Index in Table 25. According to Vanguard's website, only four outperformed the S&P 500 Index over ten years *before fees* were factored in. These four mutual funds are:

---

52.   "Mutual Funds, IRAS, Etfs, 401(k) Plans, and More." Vanguard, accessed June 30, 2022. https://investor.vanguard.com/corporate-portal/.

Vanguard Mutual Fund	10-Year Return Before Fees	Expense Ratio/Fees
Growth Index Fund Admiral Shares	15.22%	0.05%
US Growth Fund, Investor Shares	14.49%	0.38%
Growth and Income Fund, Investor Shares	14.42%	0.32%
Tax-Managed Capital Appreciation Fund Admiral Shares	14.4%	0.09%
S&P 500 Index Fund Admiral Shares	14.36%	0.04%

Table 25. Vanguard Stock Mutual Funds Ten-Year Performance Comparison to the S&P 500 Index Before Fees Included (as of 12 June, 2022)

If you were researching Vanguard's funds and weren't factoring in return *after fees*, you'd likely choose one of the four mutual funds listed above. So, how do these same funds' ten-year performance compare to the S&P 500 Index *after fees* are considered? Let's incorporate fees and re-rank the funds.

Vanguard Mutual Fund	10-Year Return After Fees	Rank Before Fees Included	Rank After Fees Included
Growth Index Fund Admiral Shares	15.17%	1st	1st
S&P 500 Index Fund Admiral Shares	14.32%	5th	2nd
Tax-Managed Capital Appreciation Fund Admiral Shares	14.31%	4th	3rd
US Growth Fund, Investor Shares	14.11%	2nd	4th
Growth and Income Fund, Investor Shares	14.1%	3rd	5th

Table 26. Vanguard Stock Mutual Funds Ten-Year Performance Comparison to the S&P 500 Index After Fees Included (as of 12 June, 2022)

After factoring in fees, only ONE of Vanguard's stock mutual funds, which has an account minimum of $50,000 or less and has been around for ten years, beats the S&P 500 Index. So, if you choose to do any of your research, *it's essential to understand how an investment performs AFTER its fees are considered.*

ONE FINAL WORD OF CAUTION ON MUTUAL FUND RESEARCH

Finally, we wanted to share one final word of caution about mutual fund investment research. Many mutual fund companies offer customers access to their mutual fund's historical performance, which can usually be filtered by year-to-date, one-year, three-year, five-year, ten-year, and "since inception." Since you're a teenager or in your twenties and have forty-plus investing years ahead of you, you'll want to research a fund's long-term performance and not its three- or five-year performance. Consider funds that have been around for at least ten years, so plenty of performance data is available.

However, researching by a fund's inception date can be misleading because *every mutual fund has a different inception date.* For example, one may have an inception date of 1993 while another may have an inception date of 2003. Comparing a fund whose inception date is 1993 to one with an inception date of 2003 is *not an apples-to-apples comparison* since their inception dates are not the same. An apples-to-apples comparison would be comparing two funds' performance to an equal *period of time*. If fund #1 had an inception date of 1993 while fund #2 had an inception date of 2003, it would be an apples-to-apples comparison to compare fund #1's performance to fund #2's inception date since fund #2 has been around for a shorter period of time.

Comparing a fund's return from the same starting point is important because the stock market has had different periods of strong and poor performance. Therefore, the same periods need to be compared against each other to not give one fund an unfair advantage over another. For example, most funds created before 2008 will usually have a lower "since inception" performance than a fund created in 2009 or later. This is because any fund started in 2009 or later was not around during the 2008–09 Recession, when the S&P 500 Index had a -38.49%

return in 2008. Meanwhile, a fund created in 2009 or later does not have a poor 2008 return to bring down its "since inception" return. Thus, a fund whose inception date is 2005 will most likely be lower than a fund whose inception date is 2010 because it will likely have a horrendous 2008 return on its record. So, without doing an apples-to-apples comparison, the fund with the 2010 inception will most likely have a higher return.

The point here is that if you are going to research any mutual fund's "since inception" date that is greater than ten years, compare it against the S&P 500 Index during the same time *with fees factored in.*

What will become abundantly clear is that *the longer the length of time a mutual fund has been around, the more likely its return goes down and converges to the S&P 500 Index's or a fund's benchmark return* and, many times, *below it.* When higher fees are factored in, it's almost 100% certain that it will underperform. Sure, a fund can look great over a one-, three-, five-, or even ten-year period, but string it out far enough, and it is almost guaranteed to underperform.

We were trying to avoid diving into this much detail, but adequate thought and research have been done beforehand for you. *This is the reason why we suggest skipping research and instead go with an S&P 500 Index Fund.* As someone who has forty-plus years of investing, you or any investment professional will NOT be able to outsmart the market by either picking stocks yourself or switching between mutual funds every few years to ride a strong three- or five-year performance. *It's just not going to happen.* Save the time and energy and instead stick with an S&P 500 Index Fund.

HOW MUCH DOES UNDERPERFORMING THE MARKET COST YOU?

Let's revisit Kate from Decision 2: Invest Young. If you recall, she accumulated $1,210,777 by age sixty by investing $151,100 starting at age sixteen. Assume she ignores this book's advice of investing in an S&P 500 Index Fund and invests her money with an actively managed fund or another investment that underperforms the S&P 500 Index by 1 or 2% after fund performance and higher fees are factored in. How does that decision affect her bottom line?

	Total Investment	Account Value at 60	Value Difference
8% Annual Return (S&P 500 Index)	$151,100	$1,210,777	
7% Annual Return (1% lower annual return)	$151,100	$904,869	-$305,908
6% Annual Return (2% lower annual return)	$151,100	$680,891	-$529,886

Table 27. The Underperformance of Kate's Investment in Actively Managed Funds

Underperforming the S&P 500 Index by as little as 1% over her life results in Kate's net worth decreasing by roughly 25%, or $305,908. In addition, underperforming by 2% decreases her net worth by approximately 44%, or $529,886. She worked the same job, made the same good life choices to cut back on expenses, and saved the same amount per month. Yet, she threw a lot of it away by *choosing the wrong investment*; with a

SAD FACT: By underperforming the market by just 1% annually, Kate decreased her net worth by 25% or $305,908.

6% annual return, she could have ended up with $680,891 instead of $1,210,777.

Underperforming the market by as little as 1 or 2% makes a substantial difference over your lifetime. Higher mutual fund fees will likely cut your annual return down by 0.6–0.8%. It's that simple to remember. Most of you are investing for the long run because you are starting young. You have thirty, forty, hopefully, fifty years ahead of you to invest, and there is next to zero chance that any actively managed fund will outperform the S&P 500 Index over your forty- or fifty-year investing period. Don't spend your investment years overpaying to underperform in the market—not when there is a better alternative. Don't be a dumba$$; invest in an S&P 500 Index Fund.

ADDITIONAL S&P 500 INDEX FUND BENEFITS

Investing in S&P 500 Index Funds is simple and easy because you don't have to do anything other than open up the fund and make regular contributions. It takes fifteen minutes to open and set up. From there, all you have to do is continue working and making regular contributions and, over time, watch as the system *works for you* and *makes you money.* You make money while you sleep. You make money while you eat out. You make money while on vacation. One of our index fund accounts has over $250,000 in gains since opening it. We didn't lift a finger or do any additional work, and our investment worked for us and made us $250,000, or more than two years' worth of Adam's salary. *That's two years of free money without actually having to work.*

One final point: It is unlikely that you will lose everything investing in an S&P 500 Index Fund. Why? Because the S&P 500 Index has never gone to 0. The S&P 500 Index has had some years of steep declines throughout its history, but it has always come back and gone higher than it was before the decline. Some of you may have heard investing horror stories about people losing everything. Rest assured that nearly everyone who lost everything likely gave their money to a professional who either stole it or invested it in some risky investment or individual stock (like Enron) that went to $0. Remember, as an S&P 500 Index Fund investor, you have 100% control over your investments and are invested in the 500 largest US companies. So if one company's stock goes to $0, there still are 499 other companies to hold up its value. The S&P 500 Index may have periods of large declines, but if it does, ride it out, keep investing, and wait for it to come back. Whatever you do, *do not sell* during declines.

WHY IT IS SO HARD TO BEAT THE MARKET OVER THE LONG RUN

We talked about how nearly all investment professionals underperform the S&P 500 Index over the long run. These professionals are highly trained, so how is this possible? Here is the

You or an investment professional will beat the S&P 500 Index over your lifetime.

thing about consistently outperforming the market over the long term: *There are too many future unknowns, and it is impossible to account for all the unknowns accurately. No amount of education, planning, or strategy can fix that.* Essentially, professionals are more educated guessers than you and me, but nevertheless, they are still guessers. Sure, it's possible to "guess" correctly or get lucky and beat the S&P 500 Index over a few years; however, *guessing is not and never will be a winning strategy* over the long term.

For example, where will oil prices be next year? What about the unemployment rate or Gross Domestic Product? How about a company's cash flow or its debt level? Interest rates? Inflation? Corporate tax rates? What party will control Congress or the White House? Is China invading Taiwan? No one, and we mean no one, can always predict where things will be

> ## NOTE TO SELF
> **"**It's too hard to beat the market because there are too many unknowns to predict.**"**

in five years, three years, or even one year. Few can consistently predict where things will be *tomorrow*. Because if they could, they would have made so much money that they would no longer need to work. If the experts knew what they were doing, why didn't they all invest big in oil companies early in the COVID pandemic when oil futures traded for a negative price? Oil futures, or how much future oil sells for, went from negative during the early stages of the pandemic to an all-time high in less than two years. Many oil companies' stocks went up more than 300% in that period. Why did oil futures go from negative to all-time highs in less than two years? Some factors include domestic and global supply reduction, a hostile fossil fuel administration, supply chain issues, COVID, vaccines and therapeutics, opened economies, and a Russian invasion of Ukraine. In other words, the reasons for the oil price increase were primarily due to world events and politics and had little to do with balance sheet analysis or anything studied in business school.

Sure, anyone can make *an educated guess* based on available data, but that's about it. In December 2019, no one predicted the COVID pandemic that would spread across the world in less than three months and result in a 40% stock market decline in two months. Likewise, few foresaw the 2008–09 Great Recession, the greatest market decline in our lifetime, despite countless loans defaulted beforehand, setting off red alerts. Why? Because, again, *no one knows*. Don't believe us? Go to CNBC.com or any other stock

IMPORTANT!

The longer your investment time frame, the harder it is to beat the S&P 500 Index.

market-following website and read some major headlines. Most days, there will be one article from one expert who believes the market will rally 10%, while another article from a different expert says that the same stock is overpriced and sees a 10% decline before the year's end. Clearly, both can't be true and many times *neither is true*. We could take screenshots of thousands of wrong financial "expert" predictions from the last year, but in the interest of not embarrassing them, we won't.

Also consider analyst stock recommendations. Analysts are paid to follow industries or individual stocks and give "buy," "hold," or "sell" recommendations and future earnings predictions on individual stocks based on their research. Most of these analysts are some of the most researched professionals out there. Many analysts provide stock tips on when to buy, hold, and sell recommendations based on their research. So how can multiple analysts, whose full-time job is following certain companies, come to different opinions? How is it possible that one analyst says a stock is a strong buy while another says it's a hold or a neutral rating? Or consider all the different earnings estimates (how much money a company will make at the end of a future period). For example, Apple Inc has twenty-four analysts covering it. At the moment, one analyst has Apple's earnings estimates for the next quarter at $1.16

a share, while another analyst estimates earnings at $1.52 a share, or roughly 30% higher. So how do two professional analysts come up with such a drastic difference in a company's earnings when it's less than three months away? Answer: It's all educated *guesswork* that is based on assumptions.

So, what have we learned? First, trying to beat the market over the long term is time-consuming and *a losing strategy*, and you will most likely end up with less money. That is why we recommend low-cost S&P 500 Index Funds. As we've shown, *it's not how much you will make that matters, but rather how much less you will make than the S&P 500 Index over the long run.*

LET'S TAKE A CLOSER LOOK AT MUTUAL FUND FEES AND THEIR IMPACT ON YOUR LONG-TERM RETURN

Earlier, we mentioned that the Vanguard S&P 500 Index Admiral fund has an annual fee of 0.04%, while actively managed funds have annual fees usually at least 0.70% or higher. Fees subtract from your fund's annual return, and the higher the fees, the less money you keep. How much do fee differences account for performance over the long run? Let's compare an actively managed mutual fund, let's name it Adam's Growth Fund, and Vanguard's S&P 500 Admiral Index fund. Both Adam's Growth Fund and Vanguard's S&P 500 Index Admiral Fund have an 8% annual return. However, Adam's Growth Fund has a 0.75% annual fee, while Vanguard's S&P 500 Index Admiral Fund has a 0.04% annual fee. After factoring in fees, Adam's Growth Fund has a 7.25% return while Vanguard's S&P 500 Index Admiral Fund has a 7.96% return. If someone invests $300 a month from age twenty-three to sixty in both funds, how much would each account be worth at age sixty after fees?

Fund	Annual Fee	Value at 60	Difference
Adam's Growth Fund	0.75%	$646,875	-$134,254
Vanguard Index Fund	0.04%	$781,129	

Table 28. Adam's Growth Fund Versus Vanguard Index Fund Returns After Fees

The above chart shows that assuming the same return between both funds, investing in a 0.75% annual fee fund reduces the account balance by 18%, or $134,254 more than the Vanguard Index Fund after fees are factored in. Again, it's eye-opening that the difference between a 0.75% and 0.04% fee, which seems like "pennies" over thirty-seven years, actually reduces an investor's total return by 18%, or in this example $135,000. If an actively managed mutual fund has a higher return than an S&P 500 Index Fund to justify a higher expense ratio over the long run, then that's one thing. However, we have repeatedly seen that over thirty-plus years, nearly all actively managed funds do not beat S&P 500 Index Funds. The higher fees only eat away at your returns, costing hundreds of thousands of dollars and decreasing your future net worth.

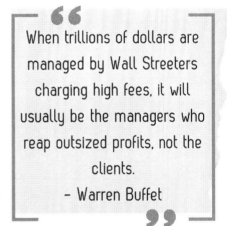

When trillions of dollars are managed by Wall Streeters charging high fees, it will usually be the managers who reap outsized profits, not the clients.

– Warren Buffet

S&P 500 INDEX FUND COMPARISON

Let's now do a side-by-side comparison of two S&P 500 Index Funds' composition, or what stocks make up the fund and the percent that each stock is of the fund's holdings or assets. For this example, let's examine the top ten holdings of Vanguard's S&P 500 Index Admiral Fund (VFIAX) and Charles Schwab's S&P 500 Index Fund (SWPPX) as of 10 June, 2022:

(VFIAX)		(SWPPX)	
Stock	**% Assets**	**Stock**	**% Assets**
Apple Inc	6.96%	Apple Inc	6.94%
Microsoft Corp	5.93%	Microsoft Corp	5.91%
Amazon	3.1%	Amazon	3.09%
Tesla	2.08%	Tesla	2.07%
Alphabet Inc	1.95%	Alphabet Inc	1.95%
Alphabet Inc	1.82%	Alphabet Inc	1.81%
Berkshire Hathaway	1.68%	Berkshire Hathaway	1.68%
Johnson & Johnson	1.35%	Johnson & Johnson	1.35%
NVIDIA Corp	1.32%	NVIDIA Corp	1.32%
Meta Platforms	1.32%	Meta Platforms	1.31%

Table 29. Top Ten Holdings of Vanguard's S&P 500 Index Fund and Charles Schwab's Index Fund Comparison

As you can see in Table 29, both index funds are nearly identical. Since the funds are nearly identical, they have nearly identical returns. So, if the funds have nearly identical composition and returns, how do we discriminate and determine which fund to invest in?

NOT ALL S&P 500 INDEX FUNDS ARE CREATED EQUAL

Now that we've established that S&P 500 Index Funds are nearly identical in composition and returns, *there is one thing that separates them. Fees.* How much do S&P 500 Index Fund fee differences decrease your return? Let's take a look. An index fund's fees are listed on its website. Typically, it's listed under a fee tab or section. The key is to find the lowest fee because index funds are nearly identical.

As we've mentioned many times already, Vanguard's S&P 500 Index Admiral Fund has an annual fee of 0.04%. In contrast, T Rowe Price's Equity Index 500 Fund, their equivalent S&P 500 Index Fund, has an annual fee of 0.18% at the time of writing this book. While the difference between 0.18% and 0.04% is even smaller than the previous example, T Rowe Price's fund charges *450% more than Vanguard's for the same thing*. Same thing, 450% higher fees. However, the difference becomes more real when you see how much less money goes into your pocket. Using the same investment strategy as in the previous example, how much would the fee difference cost someone investing $300 a month from age twenty-three to sixty, assuming an 8% annual return?

Fund	Annual Fee	Value at 60	Difference
T Rowe Price Equity Index 500 Fund	0.18%	$752,449	-$28,680
Vanguard S&P 500 Index Admiral Fund	0.04%	$781,129	

Table 30. T Rowe Price and Vanguard S&P 500 Index Fund Comparison

A 0.14% annual difference between two S&P 500 Index Funds reduces your future net worth by $28,680 or *a brand-new Toyota Camry*. It's unlikely that you would pay $4.50 for a Gatorade when you can get the exact same Gatorade at another store for $1.00. *So why would you do the same for an S&P 500 Index Fund?*

DID YOU KNOW?

Carelessly investing in a T Rowe Price over Vanguard costs you an additional $28,680, or the price of a brand-new Toyota Camry.

WHICH S&P 500 INDEX FUNDS SHOULD I INVEST IN?

As we discussed earlier, S&P 500 Index Funds are nearly identical, so it's important to find funds with the lowest fees to save yourself money in the long run. The fees are not fixed, and you are not grandfathered into the fee rate once you open it. The fees can fluctuate over time; however, fees typically go down over time and not up. So, what S&P 500 Index funds should you invest in? We'll save you some work because we already did the homework for you. At the time of this book's writing, the following S&P 500 Index Funds with the lowest fees are:

Company	Mutual Fund Symbol	Annual Fee	Minimum Investment Amount	Additional Investment Amount
Vanguard	VFIAX	0.04%	$3,000	$1
Charles Schwab	SWPPX	0.02%	$1	$1
Fidelity	FXAIX	0.015%	$1	$1

Table 31. The S&P 500 Index Funds with the Lowest Fees

Index funds, as well as all other mutual funds, also have a minimum investment amount (how much money is needed to open a fund) and an additional investment amount (the minimum required for additional investments). Table 31 captures both minimum investment and additional investment amounts for consideration. One drawback of Vanguard's Index Fund is that it requires $3,000 to open a fund, while Charles Schwab and Fidelity both require $1; hence, beginning investors will most likely not be able to afford Vanguard's high minimum investment threshold and instead go with Fidelity or Charles Schwab.

HOW DO I OPEN AN S&P 500 INDEX FUND ACCOUNT?

Opening a non-retirement S&P 500 Index Fund account is simple and takes about fifteen minutes, or about the same amount of time it takes to open a social media account. First, have your social security number and your bank information (checking account and bank routing number) available. Then, go to Vanguard.com, Schwab.com, or Fidelity.com, click on "Open an Account," and fill in all requested info. When choosing account type, select "General Investing." When asked what you want to do with dividends and distributions, select "reinvest". By doing so, your index fund's dividends and distributions will be reinvested to buy additional index fund shares. Please note that any dividends and distributions will be counted as income and will require you to pay taxes on them when filing your annual tax return.

MY S&P 500 INDEX FUND ACCOUNT IS SET UP... NOW WHAT?

Now that your S&P 500 Index Fund account is set up, continue putting as much money as you can for as long as you can. However, we'd like to provide three investing tips to increase your investing success.

Key Point 1: Importance of Long-Term Investing Perspective. The S&P 500 Index can be volatile in the short term but has had a historical average annual return of 8%. However, it doesn't return 8% every year. Some years, the returns are greater than 8%, while others are less than 8%. In addition, some years, the S&P 500 Index has a negative return, and every now and then, there may be multiple consecutive years of negative returns. When this happens, your account will temporarily go down in value as well. So, don't expect a smooth, upward trajectory. According to Bob Pisani, a correspondent for CNBC, the S&P 500 Index has had 125 declines of 5% or greater since 1946, with the quantity and severity as follows in Table 32:[53]

Decline	Number of Instances	Average Recovery Time (Months)
5-10%	84	1
10-20%	29	4
20-40%	9	14
40%+	3	58

Table 32. Quantity and Severity of S&P 500 Index Declines Since 1946[54]

However, despite several severe declines, the S&P 500 Index still has had an average annual return of 8%. Why is this important to note? Because *S&P 500 Index declines are only temporary and have*

53.   Pisani, Bob. "Long-Term Investors Shouldn't Worry Too Much about Stocks Being 10% off Their Highs." CNBC, January 25, 2022. https://www.cnbc.com/2022/01/25/long-term-investors-shouldnt-worry-too-much-about-stocks-being-10percent-off-their-highs.html.
54.   Ibid.

always recovered, and when declines do occur, they should be viewed as a buying opportunity. The S&P 500 Index came back after the early 2000s' tech bubble collapse, 9/11, the 2008–2009 Great Recession, and most recently, the February–March 2020 COVID-19 decline. Depending on the severity, it may take several months or even several years to recover, but it has always come back and gone higher. Knowing that market pullbacks are normal and that it has always recovered, it's important to *take a long-term perspective* and not panic when it occurs. Instead, when the S&P 500 Index is going through steep declines, view it as a buying opportunity and continue buying shares of your index fund because index fund purchases made during the market's steepest declines *will later become your biggest returns.*

As a young investor, you should welcome and embrace significant market declines and not let declines deter you from continually investing. Why? Because market declines allow you to buy more shares at *lower prices,* or what we like to refer to as "on sale." For example, let's say you invest $400 a month in your S&P 500 Index Fund. At the moment, your S&P 500 Index fund is currently worth $100 a share, and your $400 investment buys four shares. Twelve months later, the S&P 500 Index has dropped 25% after months of bad economic data. At this point, while others may panic and stop buying, you continue to buy. However, *you aren't a dumba$$ and understand short-term fluctuations are normal and have a long-term perspective.* You embrace market drops because you know that S&P 500 Index Funds bought during substantial declines will make you the most money when it recovers. Unafraid and having a long-term perspective, you continue buying. Your S&P 500 Index Fund shares have also declined 25% and are now selling at $75 a share. Your monthly $400 investment can now buy 5.3 shares instead of four shares like it had twelve months earlier.

Eighteen months later, the S&P 500 Index has recovered from its 25% decline after several quarters of positive economic data. Not only has the S&P 500 Index recovered, but it is now 10% higher than it was before the 25% decline and your S&P 500 Index Fund shares are now worth $110 a share. So let's take a closer look at how your returns differ based on shares bought before and during the decline.

Period	Share Price	Shares Bought	Value After Recovery ($110 a share)	Gain	Annual Return
Before 25% Stock Market Decline	$100	4	$440	+$40	4%
During 25% Stock Market Decline	$75	5.3	$583	+$183	30.5%

Table 33. Buying S&P 500 Index Shares Before and During a Decline and their Future Gains

As the table shows, the *annual return and your gains are substantially higher on shares bought during the 25% decline than when bought beforehand.* So, when these declines occur, remember this example, view it as a tremendous long-term opportunity, and continue buying. Consider buying more than you usually buy if you have additional money available, or consider temporarily cutting back on spending to free up additional money. By doing so, you will be rewarded after the market recovers. As Warren Buffet, the legendary investor and Chief Executive Officer of Berkshire Hathaway, famously said, "Be fearful (or cautious) when others are greedy (or when the market is doing well). Be greedy (or buy aggressively) when others are fearful (or during a steep market decline)."[55] Think of major stock market declines like you think of Black Friday. Everything is on sale, and the bigger the sale or steeper the S&P 500 Index is down, the more you should buy. Remember, *the*

---

55.   Brownlee, Adam P. "Warren Buffett: Be Fearful When Others Are Greedy." Investopedia, May 19 2022. https://www.investopedia.com/articles/investing/012116/warren-buffett-be-fearful-when-others-are-greedy.asp#:~:text=Warren%20Buffett%20once%20said%20that,over%2C%20and%20one%20should%20be.

S&P 500 Index has always come back, and your biggest returns come from investments made during the market's steepest declines.

Key Point 2: Timing the Market is Unrealistic. Many inexperienced investors believe that they can time the market or buy at the low point and sell at its high point. Wouldn't it be nice

> " Every decade or so, dark clouds will fill the economic skies, and they will briefly rain gold.
> – Warren Buffet "

if you or someone could consistently buy at the bottom and sell at the top? There's only one problem with that logic: No person or machine has ever cracked the magical formula, algorithm, or theory to predict it. *No one.* No one knows what the market will do tomorrow, next week, next month, or in a year. Sure, everyone has *an opinion* based on theories, assumptions, and logic, but the future is too unpredictable, and *no one knows*. Remember, the only thing guaranteed in investing is an investment's current price. Everything else is just a guess.

So, what should you do if you can't time the market? *Invest regularly.* Once or twice a month, or whenever it is shown in your budget, as discussed in Chapter 3. You can invest in one of two ways: either logging into your account each time you want to buy and submiting a buy order or setting up automatic investing. Automatic investing is where you select the day or days of each month and the amount you would like to invest. The mutual fund company will then automatically buy the investment for the amount and on the day/s of the month that is/are selected. Essentially, your investments are on autopilot, similar to an automatic monthly cell phone or car payment. If you auto-invest, you can still make additional purchases whenever you would like. So during big market declines, or when you will see your biggest returns, regularly log in and buy more to take full advantage of the sale, even if it's only $50. Unlike a pair of shoes or a TV bought on Black Friday, *an S&P 500 Index Fund never goes out of style, never gets worn out, doesn't take up closet space, and most importantly, gets more valuable as time goes on.*

Key Point 3: You Don't Have a Loss or Gain Until You Sell. Finally, the last piece of advice is understanding that you don't have a loss or gain on any investment until you sell. Until you sell, any losses or gains are only *on paper* and *temporary* and are considered *unrealized* because the loss or gain hasn't been locked in and because your investment's value can still change. For example, if your S&P 500 Index Fund is down 10%, and you hold on until the market recovers, your "10% loss" will disappear. However, once you sell, your losses or gains become *realized* and are locked in because your investment can no longer change in value as you no longer own it.

For example, let's say that in five years, your S&P 500 Index Fund is worth $40,000. Six months later, the S&P 500 Index declines 20%, and your S&P 500 Index Fund

FAKE NEWS
I've lost $10,000 because my account is down $10,000.

account is also down 20% and is now worth $32,000. At this moment, your account is *down* $8,000, but you haven't *lost* $8,000 as long you don't sell it. Once the market recovers, your $8,000 decline will disappear and your account will go back to $40,000 and even higher.

WHAT ABOUT SELLING?

Selling is complicated, and there are many opinions on when to sell. For purposes of this book, we are not going to discuss selling because your focus should be on putting as much money into your index fund as possible in your teens and twenties. That is your top priority. S&P 500 Index Funds are long-term investments, and we do not recommend selling your S&P 500 Index Fund until later in life.

WHAT ABOUT INVESTING IN INDIVIDUAL STOCKS?

Many of you may have an interest in investing in individual stocks. You may have seen *The Wolf of Wall Street* or *Greed* or maybe have heard about peers or family members investing in individual stocks. Investing in stocks appears to be easy and exciting. Leonardo DiCaprio makes a killing in *The Wolf of Wall Street*, and if he can do it, clearly it's easy and everyone can do it, right?

Before we get too excited, let's come back to reality and let logic and facts rather than emotion drive our investing decision-making. To help guide our thought process, let's look at an interesting investor performance study by the independent investment research firm Dalbar Inc. The firm studied investor performance over twenty years in actively managed mutual

IMPORTANT!

Investors are their own worst enemies.

funds and how irrational human behavior caused investors to act imprudently.[56] The study's main conclusion is that *investors are their own worst enemies when it comes to investing.*[57] The study found that short-term strategies, lack of knowledge, and discipline impacted individual investors' ability to capture long-time market benefits, which lowered long-term returns.[58] So how much did investors underperform? The study followed average equity fund investors and the S&P 500 Index from January 1, 2001 to December 31, 2020, and the results are staggering:

Investment	Annual Return	Growth of Investment	Difference
Average Active Equity Fund Investor	5.96%	$318,302	-$101,516
S&P 500 Index	7.43%	$419,818	

Table 34. Growth of $100,000 for Twenty Years with an Equity Fund Investor Versus S&P 500 Index[59]

Over twenty years, active investing underperformed the S&P 500 Index by *roughly 24%*. Ouch! This study reinforces and supports the thought that *trying to outsmart the market by picking individual stocks is a poor and losing strategy, and doing so will most likely leave you with hundreds of thousands fewer dollars in the long run.* So, don't be a dumba$$ and keep your ego out of investing. Stick with an S&P 500 index fund.

---

56.   Coleman, Murray. "Dalbar QAIB 2022: Investors Are Still Their Own Worst Enemies." Index Fund Advisors Wealth Management, April 4, 2022. https://www.ifa.com/videos/dalbar_2016_qaib_investors_still_their_worst_enemy/.

57.   Ibid.

58.   Ibid.

59.   Ibid.

RETIREMENT

Next, let's talk about a boring yet important topic that causes teenagers' and young adults' eyes to glaze over: retirement and what is needed to plan for it successfully. Why is talking about retirement important? Because the one thing that we have not been able to figure out is how to stop time and there is nothing that anyone can do to prevent aging. Whether you want to admit it or not, you will eventually get older and near retirement. The question then becomes how much money do you want to have when you retire? Because it will not only impact the kind of lifestyle you can afford, but also when you can retire.

So, how are Americans at saving for retirement? CNBC recently conducted a survey in 2021 and compiled the retirement savings for ages sixty to sixty-nine:

Percentage of Respondents	Retirement Savings
28%	Less than $50,000
10%	$50,000 to $99,000
36%	$100,000 to $500,000
14%	$500,000 to $999,000
12%	$1,000,000 or more

Table 35. Sixty to Sixty-Nine Retirement Savings

According to the survey, 74% of correspondents have $500,000 or less in retirement savings for ages sixty to sixty-nine.[60] Pause and think about that—three out of four sixty- to sixty-nine-aged adults have $500,000 or less at their retirement age. You may be thinking that $500,000 is a lot of money. However, $500,000 is not a lot to comfortably

---

60.   Elkins, Kathleen. "Here's How Much Americans Have Saved for Retirement at Different Ages." CNBC. CNBC, January 23, 2020. https://www.cnbc.com/2020/01/23/heres-how-much-americans-have-saved-for-retirement-at-different-ages.html.

live in retirement. Assuming someone retires with $500,000 at the age of sixty-five and lives to eighty years without additional income, they will have $33,333 a year, or roughly $2,788 a month, before taxes are taken out to live off. That is *not* a comfortable retirement. Healthcare costs, which are often ignored, increase as you get older and should be another consideration to think about when planning for retirement. Healthcare costs can range from zero to thousands of dollars a month depending on your age and income bracket. You may be broke during or after college, but you have forty-plus years to fix your financial future; however, there is not much you can do except work longer and lower retirement expectations once you're approaching retirement. Most people do not want to work longer than they have to.

Even more shocking is that half of *Americans don't have a retirement plan*.[61] This means half of Americans are jeopardizing retirement, resulting in many working longer than they may want to. So how do you ensure you have enough to retire? A good start is *investing as early as possible*. The various retirement investment options are in the next section. Like any other form of investment, retirement planning favors *those who plan* and *start early*.

HOW MUCH DO I NEED TO RETIRE?

It depends. There are a lot of factors when determining how much you should plan for. Two big factors include retirement age and the kind of lifestyle you want to live. Some retirement experts suggest that someone should save up enough to cover 80% of their pre-retirement income for each retirement year. Others suggest saving at least twelve

---

61.   Ibid.

times your pre-retirement income.[62] Regardless, it is likely that at least a million dollars will be needed, so starting early is critical.

INDIVIDUAL RETIREMENT ACCOUNTS–YOUR TICKET TO RETIREMENT

First, let's discuss Individual Retirement Accounts, or IRAs, which are the most popular ways for individuals to invest and save for retirement. There are two types of IRAs, Traditional and Roth, and both accounts provide special tax benefits. The biggest difference between the two is when taxes are paid. A Traditional IRA's contributions and distributions are *tax-deferred,* meaning taxes are paid *when you take out your money at retirement.* In other words, money is put in tax-free but taxed when you take the money out. Meanwhile, a Roth IRA is the exact opposite. A Roth IRA's contributions are taxed, your investments grow tax-free, and *no taxes are paid when you use it at retirement.*

FUN FACT:
Roth IRA: Money taxed going in, not taxed going out

Traditional IRA: Not taxed going in, taxed going out

---

62.   "How Much Do You Really Need to Save for Retirement?" Merrill Edge, accessed April 16, 2022. https://www.merrilledge.com/article/how-much-do-you-really-need-to-save-for-retirement.

ADDITIONAL IRA BACKGROUND INFO

When Your IRA Money Can Be Used: The soonest an IRA can be used is age fifty-nine and a half, and the latest you can begin withdrawing is age seventy. There are some exceptions to using it before age fifty-nine and a half, such as a first-time home purchase. However, using your IRA before your eligible age without an approved exemption results in a penalty and paying taxes on any gains.

Income Limitations: Roth IRAs were designed to give tax benefits and help middle- and lower-class individuals save for retirement. To do so, there is a maximum annual income limit that prevents tax advantages from benefitting upper-class individuals. The Modified Adjusted Gross Income limit in 2022 is $144,000 for single filers and $214,000 for those married and filing jointly.[63] The income limitation usually increases each year, so be sure to understand the current year's income limit.

Annual Contribution Limits. Both Roth and Traditional IRAs have annual contribution limits to limit tax revenue loss by the government. In 2022, the max Roth IRA annual contribution is $6,000 for investors ages under 50 and $7,000 for investors 50 or older. The annual contributions also change every few years, so be current on the current year's limit.

63.   Rae, David. "Roth Ira Contribution Income Limits for 2022." Forbes, January 20, 2022. https://www.forbes.com/sites/davidrae/2022/01/20/roth-ira-contribution-income-limits-for-2022/?sh=39f7246a7cbd.

WHAT SHOULD I INVEST MY IRA IN?

An IRA is simply a type of account and can be invested in anything you want: stocks, bonds, crypto, mutual funds, precious metals, etc. However, we invest our retirement in S&P 500 Index Funds because of their low fees and ability to outperform other investments in the long run. Thus, put your retirement money in an *S&P 500 Index Fund.*

SHOULD I OPEN A ROTH OR TRADITIONAL IRA?

The decision on whether you should open a Roth or Traditional IRA depends on *your current and future expected tax rates.* Your goal is to pay the least amount of taxes required by law because paying fewer taxes means more money for you. So, the easiest way to decide whether to open and invest in a Roth or Traditional IRA is to determine whether or not your tax rate is higher *today* or will be higher *in the future*. If you aren't familiar with the tax code, the United States has a progressive tax system: The more you make, the higher your tax rate is.

OPERATION DON'T BE A DUMBA$$
Your Mission:
Open a Roth IRA or
a Roth 401K.

If you think you will make less money in the future than you do today, then your tax rate is likely to be less at retirement and you should consider opening a Traditional IRA. However, if you think your tax rate is lower today than it will be in the future, then open a Roth IRA because you'll pay a lower tax rate today. Since most of you are taking your future seriously and investing young, you will almost certainly be future millionaires, and your tax rate will likely be higher in the future than today. For that reason, *we recommend opening a Roth IRA.* Both of us began investing in a Roth IRA in our twenties.

HOW DO I OPEN A ROTH IRA?

Opening a Roth IRA is almost exactly the same as opening a non-retirement account. Once you select which company and investment(s) that you want to use, follow and complete the same instructions under "Open an Account." However, select "Retirement Investing" then "Roth IRA" instead of "General Investing" for the account type. Everything else is the same, including selecting an S&P 500 Index (if that's your desired investment) and, most importantly, selecting to reinvest your dividends and distributions. Please note that all dividends and distributions earned from this account are not taxed, and you do not report this as income when filing your tax return. Also, since it's a Roth IRA, you will not pay taxes on any gains when you withdraw this money at retirement.

As discussed earlier, all Roth IRA income must be taxable income. Meaning any money put into a Roth IRA must have been taxed. For example, if you earned $3,000 of taxable income at your job, then you can put up to $3,000 into your Roth IRA with the maximum annual contribution being $6,000 in 2022 for those fifty and younger. If you earn any non-IRS-reported income such as babysitting, dog walking, or grass cutting for a neighbor that is not reported to the IRS, then that money cannot be counted or used in a Roth IRA. Remember, you have to have taxable income in order to make Roth IRA contributions.

In case you may be wondering, you are allowed to have both a General Investing S&P 500 Index Fund and a Roth IRA S&P 500 Index Fund. Whether you decide to have one or the other, or maybe both, depends on your individual circumstances and your financial goals.

WHY IT'S IMPORTANT TO LET YOUR ROTH IRA GROW UNUSED UNTIL AGE SEVENTY

As previously stated, the earliest an IRA can be used is at age fifty-nine and a half, and the maximum age is seventy. Sure, most of you may want to begin using your money as soon as possible. However, suppose someone has enough income from other sources early in retirement. In that case, it is best to let your Roth IRA continue growing tax-free as long as possible and use other money to fund retirement until age seventy. Whether that's a pension, social security, or other investments, for planning purposes, plan on not using a Roth IRA until age seventy.

How much more valuable will a Roth IRA be worth? Recall Kate's scenario from Decision 2: Invest Young. By investing in her teens, Kate accumulated $1,210,777 at age sixty. What if, instead of putting her money in a non-retirement account, Kate had put it into a Roth IRA and didn't use any until age seventy? How much more would it be worth?

Retirement Age	Value	Difference
60	$1,210,777	
70	$2,613,976	+$1,403,199

Table 36. Kate's Investment in a Roth IRA

Kate's account *doubles* by waiting an additional ten years, and she now has $2,613,976. Again, the cliché "time equals money" couldn't be more truthful in this case. If you have other sources of income in your sixties, it is recommended to let your Roth IRA continue to grow undisturbed to make a lot more by age seventy.

WHAT ABOUT 401KS?

Another retirement option besides opening an IRA is through your employer's retirement program, commonly referred to as 401Ks. These are voluntary, company-sponsored retirement programs where the employee makes predetermined contributions that are withheld from their paycheck, and the employer matches the

NOTE TO SELF

" Matching 401ks = Free Money "

employee's contribution up to a certain percentage. In addition, the employer's contribution is the employee's money to keep and take with them if they leave the company in the future. The matching contribution varies by employer, so understanding an employer's retirement program should be a factor when deciding where to work. However, it isn't uncommon for employers to match up to 5%. Some employers also offer pensions, but an employee must meet the company's minimum vesting requirements or be employed for a certain period of time. What's most appealing about matching 401Ks is it *is free money*. Let's say that again; *it is free money*. Let's look at an example to demonstrate this.

Let's say you work for an employer who matches 401Ks up to 5%. You make $4,000 a month and contribute 5% of your paycheck to your employer's 401K program, and your employer in return matches your contribution with an additional 5% for a total of 10%. In this example, $200 (or 5% of your $4,000 paycheck) is withheld from your paycheck every month, and your employer also contributes another $200 (or the company's 5% matching contribution) for a monthly contribution total of $400.

What's important to point out is that a one-for-one matching's Return on Investment (ROI), or how much you make on an investment, *is automatically 100%* because a $200 contribution immediately doubles and is worth $400 after the employer's contribution. Again, 401K matching is *free money*, and only a dumba$$ does not take full advantage of free money and does not contribute up to their employer's highest-matching amount.

WHAT TO INVEST IN?

Each company offers different investments in their 401Ks. If your employer offers S&P 500 Index Funds, like all other investments, we highly encourage investing in them because of their low fees and ability to outperform other investments in the long run. If your employer does not offer S&P 500 Index Funds in their 401K program, please reread the section earlier about how to properly research mutual funds before making your selection. Be sure to look at a fund's "since inception" performance and factor in fees. However, we do not, under any circumstances, recommend *investing in your employer's stock for risk reasons*. You wouldn't want to lose your job *and your retirement account* if your employer hits hard times.

HOW MUCH SHOULD I CONTRIBUTE TO MY EMPLOYER'S 401K?

The last and most important question is, "How much should I contribute to my employer's 401K program?" Free money is important, and we strongly encourage contributing up to your employer's maximum matching percentage. For example, if your employer matches up to 6%, contribute 6%. If your employer matches up to 4%, contribute 4%. Free money cannot be overstated because all your contributions immediately double after the company's contribution is made. We do not know of any other investment that immediately doubles other than your 401K, and it's important to take full advantage of it. If you would like to invest more in your retirement than what your employer's max matching contribution limit is, then put it in your Roth IRA.

Like IRAs, 401Ks also have annual contribution limitations, which change annually. A quick Google search will provide the current annual contribution limitations. Also, some 401Ks can be either a Roth (post-tax) or Traditional (pre-tax), similar to an IRA. Choose a Roth or Traditional 401K based on your tax situation.

I HAVE A MILLION DOLLARS... NOW WHAT?

While most of you are in the infancy stages of becoming a millionaire, here is something to consider as you begin your journey. If you follow the decisions of this book, then there is little doubt that you will become a millionaire. Let's fast forward twenty or thirty years: You make it! You're a millionaire! All your hard work pays off, literally. Now what? Do you go out and pay 100% cash on that lake house or buy those ten nice cars that you've always wanted? Maybe go to Vegas and put it all down on red? Nope. It took you twenty or thirty years to get here, so why would you blow it all in a matter of minutes?

We used a tree as a metaphor to describe how money grows. In nature, a tree eventually hits its maximum height and stops growing. However, a money tree can grow forever. There is an exception: Taking money out temporarily stunts a money tree's growth. While there are many opinions on what to do with money, we recommend letting your money tree continuously grow with minimal interference. If you want to take a branch off your money tree (use some of your money) then go ahead. However, taking it all and spending it, which is the equivalent of cutting it down, would be irresponsible.

What do most people do later in life when they don't want to be as risky with their money? They put a large portion of their money in lower-risk investments such as bonds or lower stock exposure investments and receive a fixed payout. Some lower-risk investments pay out 2 to 4%, and the owner spends the money. For example, if you had $1,000,000 and put it in an investment that yields 3%, your money tree would pay you $30,000 before taxes *every year*. No matter what you do, your million-dollar tree pays you $30,000. This money can then be used to buy whatever you want, and you never touch the principal balance or the $1,000,000. Your $1,000,000 is your boss and it pays you $30,000 without you ever having to show up to work. If you saved up $2,000,0000, then a 3% yield would pay $60,000 annually.

INFLATION AND TAXES

Finally, we wanted to conclude this chapter by discussing two important topics that impact investments and are not well-known to young investors: taxes and inflation. As stated at the beginning of the book, we did not factor in taxes throughout this book because they can be a complicated subject. We also did not discuss inflation's impact on investments but will now discuss it in this section.

TAXES

Any investor is liable to pay federal and possibly state investment gain taxes whenever a non-retirement acount investment is sold for more than what it is paid for. This book only examines federal taxes since state investment tax rates vary state to state. For example, if you buy an investment for $1,000 and sell it

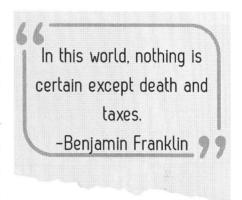

In this world, nothing is certain except death and taxes.
–Benjamin Franklin

for $1,500 then you are only taxed on your gain, which in this example is $500. Dividends are taxed at 15% for those who make between $41,675 to $459,750, while gains and distributions are taxed at either 15% or your ordinary-income rate depending on how long the investment was held. What makes investment taxes difficult, and why we did not discuss them for most of the book, is that investment taxes are not paid immediately after selling the investment, like when purchasing items in a store. Instead, your investment tax liability from gains and dividends is calculated and paid for when filing your annual tax return.

To further complicate the issue, the amount paid out of pocket on investment gains varies by year. Some years, tax deductions are enough to offset dividends and investment gains, requiring no additional taxes to be paid. Other years' tax deductions are not enough to offset your investment tax liability, and additional tax payment is required. The two investment tax scenarios are especially true for parents with childcare and child tax credits. Thus, taxes are not a clear-cut subject, and we did not include them in the book's scenarios. However, we want the reader to know that taxes exist, and your investment return will be less than what was shown in the book. How much less? We can't say for sure because everyone's tax situation is different.

Investment tax rates are dependent on how much taxable income was earned and how long the investment was owned. *Taxable income* is how much of your income is taxed, including your paychecks and investment gains. Table 37 shows the 2022 federal investment tax rates for single filers.

Item	Taxable Income	Federal Tax Rate
Dividends	$41,674 or less	0%
	$41,675 to $459,750	15%
	Over $459,750	20%
Gains		
Short-Term (owned 365 days or less)		Ordinary Income Tax Rate
Long-Term (owned 366 days or more)	$41,674 or less	0%
	$41,675 to $459,750	15%
	Over $459,750	20%

Table 37. 2022 Investment Federal Tax Rates[64]

For young investors, dividends and long-term gains are likely taxed at 0 or 15%. However, short-term gains or gains from investments held for 365 days or less are taxed at your ordinary-income tax rate, which is a higher rate and will most likely be either 22 or 24%. As can be seen, the tax code *incentivizes investors to hold their investments for at least 366 days with a lower tax rate.* Thus, keep your investments for at least 366 days to reduce your tax liability.

Before we conclude this section, we wanted to clarify that the tax rates discussed in this chapter are for non-retirement investments only.

64.   York, Erica. "2022 Tax Brackets." Tax Foundation, November 10, 2021. https://taxfoundation.org/2022-tax-brackets/.

As discussed earlier in the chapter, Roth IRA dividends and distributions are not taxable at any point since your contributions have already been taxed. Meanwhile, Traditional IRA dividends, gains, and distributions are taxed only when you pull out your money in retirement and are not taxed annually.

FEDERAL TAX EXAMPLE

Let's do a quick tax example and show how federal investment taxes are calculated. Let's say in 2022, you made $50,000 from your job, putting any additional short-term investment proceeds in the 22% tax bracket. Your non-retirement S&P 500 Index Fund is worth $40,000 and paid $350 in dividends, $200 in short-term distributions, and $400 in long-term distributions. In addition, your $15,000 Roth IRA S&P 500 Index Fund paid $131 in dividends, $75 in short-term distributions, and $150 in long-term distributions. What is your federal investment tax liability as a single filer for 2022?

Income	Amount	Tax Rate	Tax Liability
Non-Retirement S&P 500 Index Dividends	$350	15%	$52.50
Non-Retirement S&P 500 Index Short-Term Distribution	$200	22%	$44.00
Non-Retirement S&P 500 Index Long-Term Distribution	$400	15%	$60.00
Roth IRA—S&P 500 Index Dividends	$131	0%	$0
Roth IRA—S&P 500 Index Short-Term Distribution	$75	0%	$0
Roth IRA—S&P 500 Index Long-Term Distribution	$150	0%	$0
Total			$156.50

Table 38. Federal Tax Liability Example

Without factoring in deductions, your 2022 federal investment tax liability as a single filer is $156.50. In addition, you may also have to pay state taxes depending on what state you live in. As a reminder, you are only taxed on dividends, distributions, or gains (if you sell something) during the calendar year and not on the value of your investment.

I'M GETTING A RAISE... RIGHT? (INFLATION)

Have you ever heard a grandparent or a parent say how milk or some other common item used to cost less? "When I was your age, milk cost five cents." We've all heard it. That is because inflation, or the devaluing of currency, has made a product more expensive because the US Dollar's purchasing power, or

> 66
> Inflation is as violent as a mugger, as frightening as an armed robber, and as deadly as a hit man.
> –Ronald Reagan
> 99

what $1.00 can buy, goes down. Historically, inflation has been around 2% year over year, meaning that your dollar is worth $0.02 less each year than it was the year before. So, if inflation was 2%, $1.00 in 2021 is worth $0.98 in 2022, meaning you have to spend more in 2022 to get the same product in 2021. That is why the price of milk has increased since your grandparents or parents were your age.

Assuming a 2% inflation rate, $1.00 will be worth $0.83 in ten years in today's purchasing power and $0.68 in twenty years. *Having the same million-dollar buying power you have today in ten years will require $1,218,994 with 2% annual inflation.* In thirty years, a Chipotle Burrito may cost $25, and you'll be telling your kids or grandkids, "When I was your age, a Chipotle Burrito used to cost $8!"

WHAT CAUSES INFLATION?

Inflation is primarily caused by an increase in the amount of currency circulating in the economy caused by monetary policy. The dollar's value, like any other good, changes based on supply and demand. As the supply, or amount of something available, increases or becomes more available, the demand for it goes down, and so does its value. So whenever fiscal policy puts new money into the economy, it devalues the value of *your money* and all other money.

DID YOU KNOW?

With 2% inflation, you will need $1,218,994 in ten years to have the same buying power as $1,000,000 today.

During the COVID pandemic, the US government created trillions of new dollars and flooded the economy to help it. While everyone wants and enjoys free money, the ugly side effect of free money is usually inflation. As a result of flooding the economy with trillions of new dollars, the US is experiencing the highest inflation rate in almost forty years.[65] How high is inflation at the moment? In June 2022, inflation surged to 8.6% year-over-year, the fastest rate since 1981.[66] This means that since June 2021, many common goods and services

---

65.   Cox, Jeff. "Inflation Surged 6.8% in November, Even More than Expected, to Fastest Rate since 1982." CNBC, December 10, 2021. https://www.cnbc.com/2021/12/10/consumer-price-index-november-2021.html.
66.   Rockeman, Olivia. "US Inflation Quickens to 40-Year High, Pressuring Fed and Biden." Bloomberg, June 10, 2022. https://www.bloomberg.com/news/articles/2022-06-10/us-inflation-unexpectedly-accelerates-to-40-year-high-of-8-6.

are now 8.6% more expensive than they were a year ago. In other words, $1.00 in June 2021 is now worth $0.914. You may have wondered why prices were higher in 2022 at the grocery store, while ordering a pizza, or while shopping, and it's due to inflation, or the increase of currency circulation in the economy.

! IMPORTANT! !

$1.00 in June 2021 was worth $0.91 in June 2022.

INFLATION AND INVESTMENTS

Just as it's important to be aware of tax rates, it's also important to understand inflation and its impact on your investments. *Inflation doesn't just make the money in your pocket less valuable but almost makes your investments less valuable.* What's most important is understanding your investment return *after inflation*. Throughout this book, we used an 8% annual return for the S&P 500 Index; however, *the actual or real return is 6%* when factoring in 2% inflation because inflation subtracts from your return. In other words, an 8% return with 2% inflation means that you "made" 6% in real increased purchasing power. However, if

DID YOU KNOW?

With 2% inflation, you will need $2,208,040 in forty years to have the same buying power as a million dollars today.

inflation is higher, say it was 8% year over year, and the S&P 500 index had an 8% return, then the real return was 0% because high inflation negated your return. See Table 39 for different S&P 500 Index returns and how inflation impacts its real return.

Annual S&P 500 Index Return	Year-over-Year Inflation Rate	Real Return
10%	2%	8%
14%	8%	6%
-18%	6%	-24%

Table 39. Different S&P 500 Index Returns and Inflation Impacts

Remember, if inflation devalues your money by 2% a year, you will need at least 2% to offset it and break even. So, not only do you have to pay taxes on your investment gains, but you also have to offset inflation.

Because inflation subtracts 2% from your investments annually on average, it's important to include its impact on your future net worth calculations. It doesn't make sense to ignore inflation and be under a false pretense. You'll only be disappointed later in life when you realize that while your investments are more, inflation has made your money and investments worth less than you thought. To be realistic and understand your real return, *use 6% return in your calculations.* For example, Kate was worth $789,537 at age sixty by investing $300 a month from age twenty-three to sixty. However, that was assuming no inflation. With inflation eating away at 2% each year and using a 6% annual to account for inflation, Kate's future net worth in today's dollars is $514,794. Sucks, doesn't it?

NOTE TO SELF

" Use a 6% annual return to factor in inflation. "

While this may not be as encouraging as you had hoped, you must understand inflation and its impact on your future. The biggest takeaway is understanding what inflation is, what it means to your future, and how to plan for it.

Periods of high inflation hurts everybody, but it hits low-income and retirees especially hard. Retirees are hit hard because most of their investments are in fixed income or a lower-risk investment with a fixed return, which usually cannot keep up in periods of high inflation. As a result, retirees get poorer during periods of high inflation because their investments cannot keep up with inflation and their money is worth less. For example, during the current 8.6% year-over-year inflation period, a retiree with $1,000,000 invested in a 3% fixed income investment earns $30,000 annually. However, inflation reduces the value of their million dollars by $86,000, so a retiree *loses $56,000* because inflation is higher than the fixed income return. On the other hand, stocks or stock mutual funds have historically outpaced inflation over the long run because companies raise prices to offset inflation costs. This is why all investors, including retirees, should always own some stocks or stock mutual funds in their portfolio.

Lastly, let's talk about why being too conservative with your money at a young age is a bad idea. First, Certificates of Deposits (CDs) or savings accounts should only be used as a temporary place to hold your money because inflation takes away 2% of your investment's value each year. *You need something higher than the inflation rate to make a real return.*

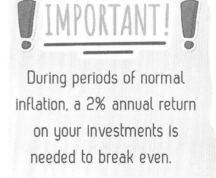

IMPORTANT!

During periods of normal inflation, a 2% annual return on your investments is needed to break even.

CDs' and savings accounts' interest may not always be higher than the inflation rate. Let's say you have money in a savings account that pays 1% interest, but the inflation rate is 8.6%. In reality, you are actually losing 7.6% and are making yourself poorer. *Bottom line, for planning purposes and during average inflation periods, you must make at least a 2% annual return just to break even in your investments;* however, inflation varies from year to year, so you must factor it in when calculating your actual wealth growth.

FACTORING IN INFLATION "RAISES" AND PROMOTION PAY INCREASES

Some of you may be reading about inflation for the first time and becoming discouraged from investing. Kate would need $2,080,685 at age sixty to have the purchasing power of $1,000,000 in today's dollars with 2% inflation at age 23. In Chapter 2's Scenario 2, you may recall that Kate invested $300 a month from age twenty-three to sixty and earned $789,537. You may be saying that Kate isn't anywhere near having a million dollars in future purchasing power. That's true; however, many employers provide annual pay raises to help against inflation and also provide job promotions or non-inflation-related, organic pay raises. So, let's do a calculation that factors both in. How much would Kate have at sixty if she receives a 2% annual pay increase to offset inflation and receives a 5% pay raise from a promotion every three years from age twenty-three to sixty and increases her monthly investments by the same percent?

	Value at Age 60
Investing $300/Month from 23-60 from Chapter 2, Scenario 2	$789,537
Investing $300/Month with 2% Annual Inflation Pay Raise and 5% Promotion Pay Raises Included from 23-60	$1,270,631

Table 40. Investment Value at Sixty with Inflation and Pay Raises Included

As the table shows, when promotion and annual inflation pay increases are included, Kate's net worth increases by 61%. So, while inflation goes up and eats away at the value of your money, your pay should increase to provide financial relief.

IS INFLATION ALWAYS BAD?

NOTE TO SELF

If the percent of my raise is less than the inflation rate, then I am getting poorer.

If the percent of my raise is more than the inflation rate, then I am getting a raise.

Inflation may have some benefits for national debt payment, but it usually harms individuals in the short term. When judging inflation's impact on your financial situation, it's important to compare it to your pay raise. For example, Adam used to get excited when the Department of Defense would release the following year's pay charts which typically showed around a 2% pay increase. "I'm making more money next year because my paycheck will be higher!" he would excitingly say. However, he later discovered that his "raise" was keeping pace with inflation, and in reality, there was no change to his purchasing power. The only time he's received a real raise was a promotion to the next rank. So, it's important to compare your hourly pay or salary raise to inflation. *If your raise is less than the inflation rate, you are getting poorer, and if your raise is greater than the inflation rate, then you are receiving a raise.*

However, in June 2022, inflation was up 8.6% year over year, and many did not receive an 8.6% raise. As a result, those people got poorer. For example, in 2022, Adam's base pay went from $8,486 to $8,715 a month, or what appears to be a nice $229 monthly pay raise. However, during the same time period,

> **SAD FACT:**
> Adam took a $501 monthly pay cut in 2022 due to forty-year high inflation

inflation was 8.6%, and his base pay needed to increase by $730 a month to keep up with inflation. Since his 2022 salary was less than the year-over-year inflation rate, *Adam actually took a $501 monthly pay cut.* To keep the family budget balanced to account for inflation, we will have to either cut $501 from spending or lower our monthly investments. Neither option is ideal; however, balancing your budget is paramount, and to do so sometimes requires actions that you would typically not prefer doing. Hence, consider *inflation as a tax* because it makes your money worth less *if you don't receive a raise big enough to offset it.*

KEY TAKEAWAYS OF DECISION 6:

- Invest in low-cost S&P 500 Index funds
- Trying to beat the market over the long run is a losing strategy
- 90% of actively managed mutual funds do not beat the S&P 500 index over ten years
- Plan for retirement as early as possible and invest in a Roth IRA
- Take advantage of free money with matching 401ks
- Understand how inflation and taxes work and affect your investments

So, the next time you get excited that you are getting a pay raise, be sure to compare it against inflation and verify that you are actually receiving a pay raise. Otherwise, it is only a mirage.

Investing can be overwhelming, complicated, and confusing. However, we hope this chapter eased any anxiety and fear about investing, and you now view investing as straightforward. In roughly fifteen minutes, you can be all ready to invest. The only other thing you have to do is continue making smart decisions day after day, month after month, and year after year to have money to invest and let the system *make you money*. We think investing is the easiest of all decisions and having the discipline to have money to invest consistently is the most challenging decision. So, we leave you with this: aggressively **budget money** and make **smart life choices** so you have money at the end of the month to **invest** in low-cost **S&P 500 Index Funds**.

This, as we said, is not an easy road. It will take your commitment, discipline, and constant effort if you want to be a millionaire. But the good news is once you commit and change your behavior, it becomes part of who you are. You become the one person everyone asks about their retirement decisions and investments because you are money smart. You are the financially literate one. You are the one who is a millionaire and have the knowledge that others seek. So, when people ask you for your advice, you'll just say, "Becoming a millionaire comes down to three things: *when you start, how much you invest, and what you invest in.*"

CONCLUSION

"Like most of you, I graduated high school proficient in reading, writing, and math but was clueless when applying my classroom education to real-life issues such as jobs, money, and investing. Neither high school nor college taught me how to connect the dots between what was taught in the classroom and problems I faced in real life. So, while I am forever grateful to all my teachers, I am puzzled why personal finance and investing were not a priority in education twenty years ago and, for the most part, remain so until this day. And by a priority, I'm not talking about taking one half-ass money-management class taught by a teacher who drew the short straw during your senior year to check a state requirement box. In my opinion, money management and the material discussed in this book is just as, if not more important than, science, English, and math. After all, no matter who you are or what you become, everyone makes numerous money decisions daily and needs to understand those decisions' second- and third-order effects. So, awareness and education are essential. The same cannot be said about other subjects taught in school, yet these subjects are readily offered and often required at nearly every school. It's unfortunate that today, finances and investing continue to be as unfamiliar to most high school graduates as an S&P 500 Index Fund or how investment professionals underperform the S&P 500 Index in the long run.

In high school, I wanted to attend college, have a successful career, and have nicer things someday. I also knew that I wanted to get married and have kids at some point, but that was the extent of my future thinking. I was told that getting good grades and a good education was essential to achieving my dreams. While that's partially true, what else needs to happen? I, and many others, graduated high school **unaware of how decisions and actions made over the next ten years would profoundly impact the amount of money we could accumulate.** *Every year that goes by without investing decreases your chances of becoming a millionaire. Your chances are heavily stacked against you if you wait until thirty.*

It wasn't until I was twenty that Jim Storandt's comment about needing $500,000 to own Buffalo County hunting land turned on a light and forever altered my thinking. That conversation may have been one of the most influential, life-changing talks I've ever had, and I will be forever grateful to Jim for it. Who would have thought that such a simple statement could become so powerful? As someone who loves deer hunting, I knew I had to do something, or I risked not hunting somewhere that was very special to me. Jim's statement ignited a spark that transformed me from a financially clueless college kid who was going through the academic motions to someone motivated to save up enough money to buy land. I began studying and researching ways to afford something, many times my future salary. I soon discovered that capitalism was, as the former Kudlow Report *show host, Larry Kudlow, always says, 'the best path to prosperity,' and was my ticket to achieving my financial goal.*[67] **It was how someone from the lower or middle class like**

---

67.   Kudlow, Larry. "Free Market Capitalism Is Still the Best Path to Prosperity." National Review, February 14, 2007. https://www.nationalreview.com/kudlows-money-politics/free-market-capitalism-still-best-path-prosperity-larry-kudlow/.

myself could become part of the upper class and how I would be able to afford something that I otherwise couldn't.

*I am a firm believer in and cannot overstate the importance of creating your net worth forecasts. Especially when you first start, because it kept me determined and motivated when everything seemed so far away. It was a constant reminder and helped me understand why I was doing it. My research and net worth analysis showed that not only could I become a millionaire but a **multi-millionaire** because I was twenty years old and had a clean financial slate. How many millions would be a function of how disciplined I was and hard I worked at it. My financial sky was truly the limit because I began in my early twenties; **your** financial sky is just as high and bright **if you choose to act.***

*So, I slowly began looking at life differently. Money's purpose was no longer solely meant to be spent, but it was meant to be spent and invested: spend some for now, invest some for **a lot more later**. I now had a defined purpose and was determined to succeed. My life and financial habits began changing as I embarked on my new path. I soon started officiating sports for additional income and automatically invested $50 monthly in a non-retirement mutual fund. While I started out by 'only' investing $50 a month, the discipline needed to pay myself first and set money aside consistently was worth its weight in gold and has stayed with me since then. Following the same lessons told in this book, those baby steps taken in early college eventually brought me to where I am today. **Everyone has to start somewhere, even if it's $50 a month while working part-time in high school or college.***

Reflecting on the journey, I now realize that grades were not as critical to my financial success as what I had been told. Money smarts and book smarts are entirely different. Book smarts are reading, memorizing, and regurgitating in a controlled environment. Money smart is mindset and attitude in a dynamic environment. Just because you are book smart or have high grades does not mean that you will be money smart or even be a millionaire because they are completely different skill sets. I know

NOTE TO SELF

" Book smarts is reading, memorizing, and regurgitating. Money smarts is mindset and attitude. "

*several people who did very well in school and have high-paying jobs but are financial trainwrecks because they spend every penny they earn. So, regardless of how much your paycheck is, it's difficult to be financially successful if you are not money smart. Sure, you have to have good enough grades to get accepted into a program or college and graduate, but that's about it. After graduation, few care about your grades or where you went to school. I'll let you in on a little secret; other than applying to graduate school, I have never been asked what my GPA was in 15 years. Grades may get you your first interview or job, but then it's all on you and how well you do at your job. I did well in high school, and my book smarts got me my first job in the Air Force. However, **my money smarts made me a millionaire.** What set me apart and led to my success were my **ambitions, patience, and unwavering drive and determination, or what I like to call a person's intangible and unmeasurable qualities.** These qualities never show up on a report card or college transcript, and it's important to know that **you are more than what's on a piece of paper.***

Like Heather, I have been asked whether the experience was worth it. There is no question that hardships were experienced along the way. However, hardships test character, and overcoming adversity provides personal growth, something we all need more

> The most important quality for an investor is temperament, not intellect.
> –Warren Buffet

of. I am grateful for the experience for two reasons. First, Heather and I have a better financial future and can hopefully provide our children with a better financial life than we had. Second, and more importantly, the experience helped me grow as a man, father, husband, and citizen.

Did I 'miss out' on a lot by living modestly because I didn't drive a nice car, wear the trendiest clothes, eat lunch out with friends regularly, or haven't been to the seven continents? No. To this day, I have no regrets. The transition from a college student to the Air Force was reasonably easy because I was already used to living a modest, college lifestyle. I didn't let my recently-acquired 'real job' paycheck drastically alter my lifestyle. I continued wearing the same clothes and driving the same car as in college. However, I could now afford Chipotle instead of Ramen Noodles and could afford to live in my own place instead of sharing an apartment or house with multiple roommates. Other than that, my lifestyle mostly stayed the same; This modest living of minimal expenses and maximum investments mentality has been with me since Jim and I went on our drive looking for deer over eighteen years ago.

Nothing *discussed in this book is difficult in concept. In fact, I would argue that Algebra I is more challenging to understand than personal finance or investing. Successful personal finance is rather quite simple:* **spend less and invest more, especially in your teens and twenties.** *What makes it difficult is convincing a teenager or young adult to set aside the lifestyle that social media and marketing 'tells' and 'expects' you to live and instead pursue something more modest. In addition, it's also challenging to convince them that the journey is worth it and to stick with it… day after day, year after year when many others are not doing the same. This is why your money skills, or mindset and attitude, are so critical because of the long-term commitment required.*

I have only been outside the United States on vacation once in fifteen years, but honestly, **who cares?** *Maybe I don't have a picture of Heather and me standing under the Eiffel Tower or drinking wine in Napa Valley in a frame in our house. Again,* **who cares?** *I still wear the same jeans I did in college. Again,* **who cares?** *Materialistic items do not define who you are as a person. My friends and family cared for me regardless of what car I drove or the price tag of my shoes. Sure, my mom would get embarrassed when riding in the paint-faded Nissan Sentra, but it never stopped her or anyone from visiting (that I know of). Likewise, wearing my mid-2000s college jeans from Express never prevented me from eating at restaurants, flying on airplanes, or shopping in stores. Nor did it prevent me from meeting and marrying Heather. As a result of my choices, I decided to live* **a materialistically poor but investment-rich** *lifestyle for my twenties and thirties, and the results have* **exceeded my initial expectations and will for you, too.**

So why did I do all this? Because at the age of thirty-eight, Heather and I no longer have to worry about investing because we followed the decisions in this book: **make it a goal, stick to a budget, choose a marketable career with as little debt as possible, buy needs instead of wants, and invest in S&P 500 Index Funds while young.** *This is a recipe that anyone can replicate regardless of their socioeconomic status. So think beyond what's important today and instead think about what will be important* **tomorrow.**

What is my "Buffalo County land" goal?

POINT TO PONDER

I know that I rambled on above, but let me conclude by asking, **what is 'your Buffalo County hunting land' goal?** *What motivates you to work hard in the classroom or take an extra shift at your job? Maybe you're working hard because you'd like to own your own business someday. Maybe you're working hard because you'd like to own a lake house someday. Maybe you don't know or can't think of anything now, but one day you will. And when that day arrives, you'll be glad that you made the right choices today because buying it will be much easier. Whatever your hopes and dreams may be,* **I hope this book made you look at life differently,** *especially with decision-making in your teens and twenties and its impact on your future. Maybe this book was your wake-up call to look at life differently; maybe it was your 'drive with Jim' moment.*

Don't let the naysayers tell you that you can't financially achieve something because of your profession, grades, education level, or whether or not you went to college. We live in a country where **our decisions and dedication matter more than our last** *name or who our parents are. By living in the freest and most opportunistic country on Earth, you can financially achieve nearly anything you want. But remember, the key is making good decisions starting in your teens and twenties and not being a dumba$$.* **Failing to make the smart decisions now will most likely result in playing catch up for the rest of your life.** *Sadly, many who fall behind will most likely never catch up...” -Adam*

Well, that's it. You now know the secret to becoming a millionaire is to *make good decisions in your teens and twenties* driven by three inputs: *when you start, how much you invest,* and *what you invest in.* The book's six decisions—make it your goal, invest young, budget, choose a marketable career, buy needs instead of wants, and invest in S&P 500 Index Funds—drive the three inputs. What brings all this together? Why does it matter? Why are these the six that make a difference? Because starting a profitable **career** with **little to no debt** allows you to **invest in S&P 500 Index Funds while young. Buying needs instead of wants** controls spending, allowing you to continue investing into your thirties while your **budget** provides the financial roadmap that guides you at all times. Finally, **making it your goal** to become a millionaire provides purpose and motivation to get started and stay with you throughout the process.

If you were hoping for a secret “how to become a millionaire” formula or a “get rich quick scheme,” then we are sorry to disappoint you. There is no fast, easy, and guaranteed drive-through option to becoming a millionaire; if you want it, you must take the time to go to the counter

IMPORTANT!

Time is the most powerful weapon in your investing arsenal.

and order. However, since *everyone* can make good decisions, *everyone can be a millionaire.* There is no person or system that is preventing you from achieving it or oppressing your efforts; *it is up to you,* and *only you can make it happen.*

WHY IS BECOMING A MILLIONAIRE DIFFICULT?

As discussed earlier, we believe there are two primary reasons why Americans might struggle to become millionaires. First, many people struggle with the concept of *wants versus needs.* To be extreme, people need three things to survive: food, water, and shelter. *Everything else is just a want.* Yes, this is a radical way of looking at things, but the fundamental issue is that Americans have a spending problem. Americans buy way more wants than needs and burn through a lot of money doing so. So instead, focus on making smart decisions today that impact your future. But that is the challenge. That is the hard part—to see a future past today and tomorrow, past the fancy coffee drinks and nights out on the town, past the decisions you make today and what they mean for your future.

By no means are we saying that you should not buy or own nice things in your life. By no means are we saying that you should spend all your time isolated in your apartment eating Ramen Noodles to invest a few more dollars. Instead, we urge you to live *modestly* in your teens and twenties and invest as much as possible. Believe it

> "Someone is sitting in the shade today because someone planted a tree a long time ago.
> –Warren Buffet"

or not, you can have fun without blowing your spending despite what marketing tells you. What you own or buy *does not define who you are.* Instead, buy your needs and invest as much as possible to have enough money for your wants later. There is no question that this requires a shift in mindset and deprogramming your thinking with everything corporate marketing has told you for your entire life. You *can* be a great athlete without buying Nike clothing. You *can* meet a great girl or guy without a fancy car or wearing the latest fashion fad. Those who figure this out are destined to be millionaires. Remember, every time you buy something, you make *someone else* rich and help *their* future. Stop making others rich and instead focus on yourself and *your* future by paying yourself first.

Second, many people lack financial education or even simple money awareness. They are unaware that investing small amounts of money a month in their teens and twenties will be worth a lot of money. Some believe the system is rigged. *If teens and young adults fully understood their financial potential, many would alter their spending and money habits at this very moment.* They are unaware that *anyone* can be a millionaire and that the "impossible" is actually very much possible. They think large amounts of wealth are only obtainable for doctors, lawyers, and professional athletes—not teachers, firefighters, electricians, personal trainers, and military personnel. However, this book demonstrates that this is not the case and that anyone can be a millionaire regardless of profession if certain steps are taken. They think it can never happen because the odds and the system is rigged and stacked against them. Well, it is possible. It is

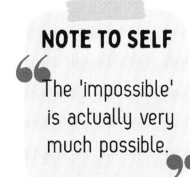

NOTE TO SELF

"The 'impossible' is actually very much possible."

attainable. And the only odds against you are the ones you create and perpetuate yourself by making poor decisions. You decided to date your boyfriend or girlfriend who has expensive taste. You decided to attend an out-of-state or private university without any financial assistance or scholarships. You decided to buy an expensive car at twenty-two.

Like you, we were both unaware because we had never received any financial education in school. We never knew that the decisions made in our teens and twenties would have profound financial impacts on the rest of our lives. We had no idea that the younger you start, the more you will have. Rather than saying, "It will never happen," we both said, "*How can we make it happen?*" Rather than accepting the impossible, we thought of a way to make it possible. But, we wanted it, we worked for it, and made smart choices to achieve it.

In the end, *you are where you are today based on decisions made in the past, and you will be where you are in the future based on today's decisions. Or said in another way, to have a better and more prosperous tomorrow requires better decisions today.* Now is when you make being a millionaire not just a dream but *your goal* and therefore make it a reality. *Your timing couldn't be better.*

IMPORTANT!

To have a better tomorrow requires better decisions today.

In summary, this book provided all the information necessary to be financially successful. Now *it's your turn to execute.* You are the ideal millionaire candidate with the highest probability of achieving it because you are young and have a clean financial slate. Avoid starting your journey by digging yourself into a substantial financial hole. Avoid large student loan debt for a degree or training program that doesn't pay for itself or buying an expensive

FAKE NEWS

I cannot become a millionaire.

car. Avoid charging things to your credit card that cannot be fully paid off at the end of the month. Becoming a millionaire is by no means easy. In fact, we never claimed this was easy. We only claimed becoming a millionaire is a straightforward process with three inputs—*when you start, how much you invest, and what you invest in*—that are influenced by six decisions. These inputs are in your control, and only you can make it happen. Of course, short-term bumps and inconveniences will happen; however, when inconveniences occur, go back to the basics: Make. Smart. Decisions. Choose to pay yourself first, especially while young. Choose to invest in your financial freedom. Choose to be a millionaire. And most importantly, don't be a dumba$$!

OPERATION DON'T BE A DUMBA$$

Your Mission:
From this point forward,
Don't be a Dumba$$!

APPENDIX

(quotes from the book citations)

Page 1   Graphic: "A Quote by Mohammad Ali." Goodreads. Accessed October 5, 2022. https://www. goodreads.com/ quotes/121663-impossible-is-just-a-bigword-thrown-around-by-small.

Page 19   Graphic: Robbins, Tony. "Tony Robbins Quotes, Read These Famous Quotes from Tony Robbins." tonyrobbins.com. Accessed October 5, 2022. https://www.tonyrobbins.com/ tony-robbins-quotes/#:~:text=%E2%80%9CSetting%20 goals%20is%20the%20first,the%20challenges%20that%20 may%20appear.%E2%80%9D.

Page 22   Graphic: Schuller, Robert H. *Tough Times Never Last, but Tough People Do!* Hardcover ed. Nashville: Thomas Nelson Publishers, 2005.

Page 28   Graphic: "Warren Buffett Quotes." Warren Buffett quotes. Accessed October 5, 2022. http://www.notablequotes.com/b/ buffett_warren.html#:~:text=I%20made%20my%20first%20 investment,my%20life%20up%20until%20then.

Page 32   Graphic: Jackson, Curtis J. "Compound Interest: 'The Eighth Wonder of the World': Business." Architeuthis Dux. April 16, 2021. https://architeuthis-dux.org/compound-interest-the-eighth-wonder-of-the-world-business/.

Page 50 Graphic: Murphy, Sean. "Paul Saffo at Churchill Club Breakfast Tue Aug 28." SKMurphy, Inc. December 8, 2015. https://www.skmurphy.com/blog/2007/08/14/paul-saffo-at-churchill-club-breakfast-tue-aug-28/.

Page 51 Graphic: "Norton Cuban Quote: 'Today Is the Youngest You Will Ever Be. Live like It.'" Quotefancy. Accessed May 16, 2022. https://quotefancy.com/quote/1151916/Mark-Cuban-Today-is-the-youngest-you-will-ever-be-Live-like-it.

Page 59 Graphic: "A Quote by Warren Buffett." Goodreads. Accessed May 17, 2022. https://www.goodreads.com/quotes/7374491-do-not-save-what-is-left-after-spending-instead-spend.

Page 71 Graphic: "A Quote by Stephen R. Covey." Goodreads. Accessed May 16, 2022. https://www.goodreads.com/quotes/104483-i-am-not-a-product-of-my-circumstances-i-am.

Page 80 Graphic: "Student Loan Bankruptcy." Student Loan Borrowers Assistance. Accessed May 17, 2022. https://www.studentloanborrowerassistance.org/bankruptcy/#:~:text=If%20you%20can%20successfully%20prove,court%20to%20start%20collecting%20again.

Page 107 Graphic: "78 Money Quotes to Make You Wealthier." Getchip. November 3, 2021. https://getchip.com/money-quotes/.

Page 114 Graphic: "25 Life-Changing Money Quotes to Save More and Spend Wisely." Our Mindful Life. April 14, 2022. https://www.ourmindfullife.com/save-money-quotes/.

Page 116 Graphic: "A Quote by Steve Martin." Goodreads. Accessed May 16, 2022. https://www.goodreads.com/quotes/273227-i-love-money-i-love-everything-about-it-i-bought.

Page 122   Graphic: Svoboda, Martin. "Americanism: Using Money You Haven't Earned to Buy Things…" Quotepark.com. Accessed May 16, 2022. https://quotepark.com/quotes/2112992-robert-quillen-americanism-using-money-you-havent-earned-to-buy/.

Page 131   Graphic: Ruth, Angela. "Paul Samuelson - Investing Is like Watching Grass Grow." February 19, 2021. https://due.com/blog/paul-samuelson-investing-is-like-watching-grass-grow/.

Page 135   Graphic: "Robert G. Allen Quotes." BrainyQuote. Accessed May 16, 2022. https://www.brainyquote.com/quotes/robert_g_allen_190121.

Page 141   Graphic: Wattles, Jackie. "Warren Buffett Beat the Hedge Funds. Here's What He Learned." CNNBusiness. February 28, 2018. https://money.cnn.com/2018/02/24/investing/warren-buffett-annual-letter-hedge-fund-bet/index.html.

Page 152   Graphic: "25 Life-Changing Money Quotes to Save More and Spend Wisely." Our Mindful Life. April 14, 2022. https://www.ourmindfullife.com/save-money-quotes/.

Page 160   Graphic- Holodny, Elena. "Warren Buffett: 'Every Decade or so, Dark Clouds Will Fill the Economic Skies, and They Will Briefly Rain Gold.'" Business Insider. February 25, 2017. https://www.businessinsider.com/warren-buffett-fear-is-your-friend-2017-2.

Page 175   Graphic: "Benjamin Franklin's Last Great Quote and the Constitution." National Constitution Center. Accessed May 16, 2022. https://constitutioncenter.org/blog/benjamin-franklins-last-great-quote-and-the-constitution.

Page 178   Graphic: "Ronald Reagan Quotes." BrainyQuote. Accessed May 16, 2022. https://www.brainyquote.com/quotes/ronald_reagan_125910.

Page 187   Graphic: "Affirmation Mondays 226 – You're Always One Decision Away from a Totally Different Life." Lawhimsy. January 31, 2022. https://lawhimsy.com/2018/11/12/monday-mantra-226-youre-always-one-decision-away-from-a-totally-different-life/.

Page 191   Graphic: Dzombak, Dan. "25 Best Warren Buffett Quotes." The Motley Fool. The Motley Fool. September 28, 2018. https://www.fool.com/investing/general/2014/09/28/25-best-warren-buffett-quotes.aspx.

Page 195   Graphic: "Warren Buffett Quote." Lib Quotes. Accessed May 17, 2022. https://libquotes.com/warren-buffett/quote/lbv3b3a.

Made in the USA
Monee, IL
22 December 2022